Rainbows in Dreams

PARAMESH DUTTA

Rainbows

in

Dreams

By

Paramesh Dutta

Originally published in India

ISBN: 978-93-89540-62-8 (Paperback)
978-93-89540-63-5 (eBook)

Published by RIGI PUBLICATION

777, Street no.9, Krishna Nagar Khanna-141401 (Punjab), India

Website: www.rigipublication.com

Email: info@rigipublication.com

Phone: +91-9357710014, +91-9465468291

PREFACE

Today the people have to be more competitive to achieve success in life. This situation has by and large compelled them to be a little selfish. In the process the parents and their own people living in the villages are facing extreme loneliness and desolation. The living style of the people are increasingly becoming materialistic. The people are made to believe that happiness can be acquired by money. In the run for name and fame many people end up with severe frustration. Craving for personal comfort has seriously affected the age old family bonding in our society.

In this scenario Dr. Nandita a qualified doctor opted to steer her life against the current social norms and decided to sacrifice all her personal aspirations and future comfort of life. She decided to serve the poor and the deprived people of her own place. She was determined to pursue her vision that satisfaction of soul lies in giving and not in getting.

I am thankful to Team RIGI for taking up the responsibility of publishing the book.

(1)

What's in a name? That which we call rose by any other name would smell as sweet

- William Shakespear

The Autumnal morning was creeping steadily towards day. The wind was blowing strongly. The leaves of trees crackled as though they were on fire. Govinda Kakati was relaxing in the sunny front yard of his house which was covered with grass lit up by the slant rays of the morning Sun. Time was of little importance to him. The sunlight gleamed on the tree leaves. The sparrous were twittering in the tree in the light and radiant morning The flowers were gently swaying in the breeze. There was big royal poinciane (Krishna Chura) tree just outside the eastern boundary of Kakati's home. A few desiccated leaves were lying on the courtyard. He was sitting in the shade of the tree to avoid direct dazzled sunlight. He was serving as a teacher of Barsila High School. He was the founder teacher of the school from its venture stage. For the initial ten years he served without any remuneration. After the school was provincialised by the government he was entitled to his regular pay.

His house was located about a mile away from Barsila a rural town. The compound of Kakati was large and was full of several fruit bearing trees. There was a sprawling outer lawn. One Mesua (Nahar) tree was there just near the gate. He was a fine and delicate man and widely admired by the people of the locality. The village had a very low rate of literacy and almost all residents were indigent agricultural workers. Education among the residents was of very low level. Being a learned man in the village people used to rush to him for his prudent opinion on any problems including problems of very trifling nature. His decisions were gladly accepted by the feuding parties.

His wife Nilima Kakati came with a cup of tea for her husband and urged him of taking bath early and to go the market. It was a day for the weekly market at Borsila. 'Sarubapu is already ready and waiting for you. I have given him the list of items to be brought from the market' She told.

The moment she turned back to go inside the house she sensed a sound of pulling the bamboo bars of the wicket gate. She instantly turned and saw a middle aged man drapped with a short dhoti and a shabby shirt entered liston the compound. A minor girl was by his side timidly looking at the house and was hesitating to enter. The poor man pulled her inside. Before Kakati could comprehend the situation, they came near Kakati and squatted with folded hands before him. The man directed the girl to touch Kakati's feet.

'Deuta, my lord' he sank to his feet and blurted out 'I pray you, please save me Sir,'

Kakati and wife both were completely taken a back at the unexpected scene. Kakati was sympathetic and said with a genial smile 'You look wretched, what is wrong with you? What is your problem? Get up and explain without any hesitation.'

'Sir' he plucked up the courage and said meekly in earnest submission 'Deuta, I am a share cropper from the neighbouring village Singori. My name is Hari Roy. I have a hungry family to feed sir. Meeting the both ends for my family is beyond my capacity. What ever I receive as my share from toiling other's land is not adequate even for half the year. We are suffering from acute misery. I have three daughters and two sons, I am unable to provide minimum staple to them. I beg on you to have pity on us.'

Kakati thought in his mind that the biggest problem was that the poor people are blessed with more children. 'Is she your daughter?' Kakati interrupted and asked. Not that he did not guess but he quipped just to make the conversation shorter.

The girl gazed vacuously into the space.

'Yes Sir' he pointed at her 'She is the middle one. Her name is Nandita.'

'What?' Faint sense of uneasiness flowed in his body. Kakati was lost in thought for a couple of minutes. Then he shook his head in disbelief. 'Nandita, a really good name. Do you know the meaning?

Hari gave a stupor look at Kakati. He was bewildered and nervous.

'Nandita means she who gives happiness, pleasure to others. But why have you brought her here?' Kakati explained with elation.

'Sir,' He said wheedling voice 'I pray you sir, you keep her. She will help Madam and assist her in all domestic chores like sweeping, cleaning, washing etc. It is my fervent prayer Sir. She is physically fit and has the natural capabilities to learn the required skills.'

Kakati's wife was curiously watching the entire proceedings with amusing look. She appeared to be pleased and gave them a warm glowing smile. She came near them, scanned the girl affectionately and she agreed to keep her without slightest hesitation.. Nilima was a very tender hearted lady. She was infact frantically longing for such type of a domestic maid for last several months. She found Nandita perfect to her expectation. Nilima hold Nandita's hand affectionately and looked to her husband 'She will be good. We are is need of a such type of girl as domestic help. I think we should keep her with us.' At the first sight I am convinced that she will be good.'

Kakati was also pleased but there was a gloom in his weired face. He gave Hari an apprehensive glance.

'But Hari" Kakati said with a slight hesitation. 'There is delicate a technical problem. Don't get frightened. My daughter's name is also Nandita'.

Hari sprang up suddenly. A wave of fear swept over him. 'Sir, please', he crouched down close up Kakati's feet 'Sir, please do not disappoint me. I do not need anything. My only prayer is to provide her some rice as meals. Her absence in my family will be my savings. Only because her name matches with your daughter's for God's shake don't reject her. Sir. I can not take her back. She will die of starving in my place.'

'No! No!' Kakati raised his hand and tried to reassure him. 'I am not saying that. We will keep her like our family member. There will be no discrepancy in food etc. She will be like one of my own children.' Kakati seemed thoughtful and after a short pause he looked at him and said 'I am worried about her name. Hari you had given her a very sweet and meaningful name. Would you mind if I change her name?' He was apologetic and said softly.

Hari was gratified and looked down wards. After a while he gathered some strength and said 'Sir we are ordinary riff-ruff people. Our bitter struggle is with starvation. We need food and a bit of cloth.' There was wariness in his tone and he was on the verge of tears. He deeply sighed and managed to stutter a reply. 'Sir, name means nothing to us. Name is a non issue for people like us. It doesn't help us in our life. It doesn't help remove our hunger. Sir you can call here by any name but for God's shake do not send me back empty handed.'

'But she may not like that? Her sentiment may also get hurt?' Kakati seemed to be a little worried.

'Frankly speaking sir, I had not given her that name.' Hari looked at him fervently and told with folding hands. 'We don't know all these. Our village 'Mandal' gave the name. While giving the name he also gave us a word of caution that she might not be able to keep the name for long.' After a little pause he said 'Names of my children are Bandita, Nandita, Paramita and Ranajoy and Sanjoy.'

Kakati looked at him in amazement 'Really! All are very meaningfull names. The Mandal must be a well read man.'

'Yes sir' Hari said with an appreciating smile. 'Actually Mandal is in contact with many respected people in the government. Infact he had arranged my eldest daughter to stay with one magistrate. She is there for last three years. Sir and Madam are very kind hearted. They have told me that they will arrange for her marriage with a suitable boy.'

'That's really great' Kakati nodded his head.

Hari blurt out without again 'She also lost her name and became Tagar.' After a little pause he said 'women have meaning for the people who have some identity. Beggers can't be choosers.'

Govinda Kakati looked outside and his glance went to the perennial ever green Rangood creeper (Madhabilata) and smile touched the corner of his lips. He found a close similarity of the flowing hair plaits of the girl with the creeper.

Kakati was glad and he quickly said 'alright then, we will call her Madhabi, Madhabi is a very beautiful flower with sweet scent Sister is Tagar and she will be Madhabi.'

Hari sighed with a relief and gave a contended smile. Nilima by then led Madhabi inside. Nandita glanced behind at her father with faintly frightened look. Without speaking anything she stood for a moment. She saw moisted eye of her father. She obediently followed Nilima Kakati and disappeared inside the house.

Hari then stood by and bowed low and touched his feet to beg leave. Kakati patted him on his back and said. 'Hari don't worry. She will stay here like one among us. Do visit us sometime and meet her. She will feel happy.'

Water gathered in Hari's eyes. He just left feeling gloomy without uttering any word. He had a mixed feeling of relief somewhere inside a sad heart. Hari slowly walked towards the gate.

There was a big commotion inside the house. Nandita and Debabrata were extremely jubilant to see Madhabi. They seemed to think she is a God's gift to the family. Nandita had cracked her medical entrance examination and was spending leisure time in home for a few days before joining her college. She jumped from her seat and hold her hand. Nandita's eyes were shining with excitement. Madhabi was not a girl of great beauty. She was of dark complexion and flat nosed. She was a raw portrayal of working class village girls. Nandita liked her and politely asked 'What is your name?' Madhabi was baffled, 'what to say?'. She gave a nervous glance to Nilima Kakati. Who instantly came to her help and said 'We will call her Madhabi'. That is her sobriquet. She looked down and mumbled 'Madhabi'.

Debabrata was happy with the thought that then onwards there would be at least one attendant in their home. which was exceedingly became necessary. He was concerned about his mother specially after Nandita would leave for her study in Medical College at Guwahati. Any way Madhabi was a God sent to Kakati's family.

Thus Nandita, daughter of Hari from Singori village vamished into the space and instead Madhabi emerged in the family of Kakati. A rustic girl from Singori village get transformed like a moth into a butterfly.

Nilima Kakati led Madhabi to the tubewell and taught her to wash and to take bath. She took Madhabi to familiarize every nook and corner of the house.

Nandita called Madhabi near her. Nandita felt a deep affection for her right from her first sight. Nandita put her hand around Madhabi. She was stiff and was looking at Nandita in a very strange way. Nandita said 'Don't get frightened. I am like your elder sister.'

Madhabi's eyes twinkled with amusement. Nandita gathered all information about her family. In the afternoon she took her to Barsila to buy some dresses for her.

They went to a haberdasher in the town and selected two frock pieces of different print. Nandita asked the tailor to take measurement to stitch two frocks for Madhabi.

Nandita asked her affectionately 'Are you pleased' Madhabi gave Nandita a quick glance and she nodded her head in happiness. She could not dream to get two dresses he one like that.

Within a short time Madhabi picked up every details of all domestic duties efficiently. She threw herself into the family and gradually their dependency on her increased. She was successful in making her importance felt in the family. She experienced a dreamy comfort there and considered her to be lucky that her prayers were answered by the God.

(2)

Be sure you put your feet in the right place, then stand firm

- Abraham Lincoln

People of Barsila had till then not come across with such a talking box called radio. Barsila was a small town and was lacking of modern basic amenities like electricity, sanitation and health care facilities. It had a high school and a post office and a primary health centre. The head master of the high school was the most respected man in the town. He was also quite well to do. He had large area of cultivable land. Head master bought a radio, a battery along with an antenna from Guwahati. The children were jubilant about the new addition to their house. His elder son was busy in erecting a bamboo pole outside the house to put the antenna in the top of the pole. One or two persons walking by out of curiosity inquired him about the kind of job he was doing. He explained the functions of the radio with an air of conceit. He said boasfrully 'There is no connecting wire or electricity, it will talk and sing by itself. The people looked at him with amusement. After the news spread in the residents of small sleepy town the close neighbourhood gathered to listen to the radio in their home. The house got almost packed to get the evening local news. It was an everyday rituals.

One evening the results of matriculation examination was announced in the radio. The people were listening the news as usual and paid rapt attention to get the news fresh from the oven. Because many people expected that history was likely to be scripted by Barsila that year. People expectations were far up. The names of first ten position holders were declared one by one. The gathering clapped in jubilation when name of Debabrata Kakati from Barsila High School was announced in the fifth position. The head master sprang up and exclaimed in exhilaration. Every one greeted each other. The people gathered there were upbeat and excited. Debabrata son of Gobinda Kakati of Naokori village had made this town and the school proud by securing rank among all the successful candidates in the state. Head master seemed to be overwhelmed with self esteem on such an outstanding performance of one of his students. He rose to his feet and raised his hand said 'We should go to Kakati's house and should break the news to them, without delay. Come on, lets move.' All of them were euphoric and agreed and a roar of 'Yes' filled the house.

Bipin Sarma was one of two B.Sc. teachers in the school and he who was popularly known as Bipin B.Sc. among the students and the public alike proposed that they should buy some sweets for the family as a token of his achievement. He ran to the nearby tea stall to by some sweets. Shopkeeper was initially buffled why he wanted sweet at that unusual time of night. He was ready to shut the shop. Bipin B.Sc. disclosed him the speciality of the occasion. The shop keeper was jubilant and gleefully said 'It's a proud moment for all us. I cann't take money for this. Sir, you should rather take all sweets and share among all of you.'

Bipin B.Sc. beamed and nodded with appreciation.

Head master accompanied by Bipin B.Sc. and a few people reached Gobinda Kakati's house. Night was drawing in and there was mild ripples in the air. The house was quiet and dark. The greasy light of the kerosene lantern was seen inside the house of Kakati

'Kakati' Headmaster shouted and knocked the door.

Kakati was shocked and rushed to the door. 'Sir! What the matter?' Kakati graciously opened the door. He was trying to puzzle out why they have come to his house at this odd hours in large numbers.

Head master hugged him with a gratifying expression on his face 'Your son Debabrata stood fifth among rank holders in the Matriculation examination. Congratulations.' Gobind Kakati was absolutely dumb founded. Debabrata came running near them. He was flashed with excitement at the news. Room was cluttered and everybody huddled around Debabrata to congratulate.

'We have got the news in the radio a few minutes back. Its marvellous. You have made all of us very proud.' All said in unison. Kakati sat in his chair, fears of happiness gathered in his eyes.

The News spread swiftly in the town and people were busy discussing. In the next morning visitor started pouring into Kakati's house to congratulate Debabrata and his parents.

It was an unprecedented happening and unheard by the people of entire Barsila town and for that matter for all other neighbouring villages. The town was out of gear in excitement. As expected the jubilation of the High School students and teachers knew no bounds.

The result however came as a great relief to Debabrata. There was a relentless pressure on him to excel in the examination. All those days were a stressful time for him. Finally he achieved an epic success.

Barsila high school was the only high school there. Debabrata was the brightest student of extra ordinary calibre since his childhood. His teachers recognised the potential and they held high hopes on him. Every teacher kept an eye on him and put there utmost effort all through his school days.

His parents, brother and sister all had a very tough time to attend all people gathered in their house during those couple of days with courtesy and politeness. But hidden from the view was the young maid who was serving tea and biscuits to the constant stream of visitors ceaselessly, without having any idea of the importance of the event. She heard word congratulation which was Latin for her.

Kakati was modest and diffident about his own success. He was able to earn admiration from the people of the village for his humbleness. In fact the family had no occasion of involving into any contentious matters in the society. None of the members of Kakati's family ever indulged in any deceitful conduct. His children learned politeness and moral virtues from their parents. The family was an ideal family in all respects and was very much respected in the village.

Debabrata was the youngest of three children. The eldest was Banibrata and they had a sister Nandita in between them. Banibrata was perusing his post graduate studies in Physics under Gauhati University and Nandita was studying in the Guwahati Medical College. A typical lower middle class family gifted with promising future. The children had their own vision and determination to convert their dreams into reality. It was a God's grace that each one of them had brilliant academic career. People at Barsila had lot of high expectation for them. People talked about them with lofty optimism and asked their children to imbibe Kakati's children.

Kakati's house was located about a mile away from Barsila High School. There was a big Royal poinaiana (Krishnachura) by the road side just outside their compound. It had farn like leaves and flamboyant display of scarlet red flowers during the early summer. It was also known as 'flame tree.' This was the iconic land mark of their house. Debabrata always walked bare footed to school with three other friends from the same village. During the monsoon months the path leading to the school became sticky with mud and sludge. Debabrata was never deterred by all those natural hindrances but he was very focused in his studies. His eagle eyed devotion earned praise from his teachers.

The most respected teacher of Debabrata, Bipin B.Sc. came and patted his back blessed him and said 'Deba you have made your parents, the teachers and student and above all the entire locality proud by your exceptional achievement. Society felt obligated to you. We all pray in unison to almighty to bless you in life. We hope you will be of great service to our motherland.'

'Sir', Debabrata bowed and touched his feet and mumbled with socking voice. 'Kindly keep your blessing on me always sir, no matter how much the time and distance keep us separate, blessings of my parents and teachers in particular and all well wishers in general will inspire and empower me to steer my life towards the goal. I vow to serve my society as a worthy son.'

The visitors gradually started thinning. After a few days Nandita left for Guwahati to resume her studies.

During those days everybody noticed the unbeatable spirit of Madhabi in attending the guests. She was bustling around the kitchen and made tea etc and served all of them. Her honest love and concern for the members of the family and the guests was amply evident from her indomitable tenacity. Of course everyday reciprocated with similar affection to her. She was treated by all as one of the family members of Kakati, right from the day one and she mesmerised all of them by her devotion and dedication.

The school authority organised a gathering to felicitate Debabrata for his success which was a honour to the school. Gobinda Kakati was also invited to address the gathering as a successful father. A good number of people from neighbourhood villages were invited to make the occasion a success. Teachers, students and various people who were highly euphoric formally fetted Debabrata there. Right from the Head master, teachers, students and others falicititated Debabrata with gamocha. Gobinda Kakati was very emotional and he humbled while delivering his speech. He quoted a verse from the Geeta and advised the student to follow what lord Krishna preached Arjuna that we should work diligently with ones aim in life without bothering for the result. One has be focussed without detraction. He expressed his deep sense of gratitude to all for blessing Debabrata and honouring him in presence of such an elite gathering. Almost all the teachers heaped praises to Debabrata and asked the students to emulate Debabrata to achieve success in life. Bipin B.Sc. emphasised that success can not be achieved by magic it takes sweat and hard work. He explained how minutely he went through the subject and it was a delight to teach a student like him. He felt lucky to have Debabrata as his student. Debabrata in his speech said that he was highly indebted to the teachers and expressed that the days he spent in the school would be cherished in all his life and would never wipe out from his heart. The audience broke into raptures of applause.

Three students with whom Deba used to go to school always from the village accompanied back to his house from the school. They were very emotional since they knew that very soon Deba will depart from Barsila. They were extremely happy on his remarkable achievement of their friend but on the other hand they were sad that they will miss him. They stopped under the blooming flame tree in front of Deba's house for a while. The boy who was two years junior to him gave a slight sad smile and hold his hand and said in a soaking voice "Deba da your result has delighted us and we are inspired at your success'. Water gathered in his eyes 'But part of me is sorry because you will go to the city for higher studies and we will miss you'. After a pause he said 'Whenever you come here please do meet us without fail.'

Debrata hold their hands and said with emotional voice 'Certainly, how can I forget you all. Your company will always remain as a precious treasure in any heart.'

(3)

Try not to become a man of success. Rather become a man of value

-Albert Einstein

Kakati's elder son Banibrata was studying Physics in the university. His earnings as a high school teacher was far from adequate to meet the educational expenses of all children. His daughter Nandita was in second year in the medical college. She is somehow managing her expenses from the economically backward scholarship, she got. Debabrata the younger son will appear for in Intermediate examination and IIT entrance test that year. He was studying in Cotton College. Obviously the income of Kakati was far from adequate to meet the required educational expenses. Banibrata therefore tried his best to earn his expenses by tutoring general and advance mathematic to a few school students.

Time flies and things move as designed by destiny. Debabrata cracked IIT entrance which became another feather in the cap of Barsila. Kakati sold a plot of land and also took loan from various sources during the time of his admission. He was passing through a challanging time and he had to spend every penny with utmost caution.

Both Kakati and his wife were completely dependent upon Madhabi. Nilima Kakati was almost incapacitated due to her failing health. So she had handed over the kitchen to her. Contrary to old practice Madhabi took charge of the kitchen and cooked food for them. The family discard had the compulsion to the age old customs of castism in the society. Madhabi had taken full responsibility and was able to earn dependency by her dexterity.

Kakati's home once filled up with children turned into a quiet hermitage where two old persons were spending their time in utter desolation. Kakati couple could not but to accept the fact that there would be no escape from that situation because that was the law of nature. Children grew up and they go out to build their career and get established. All parents yearn for that. At a time people build their houses and enjoy with children. But a time comes when they feel rather empty. The house gradually turned into a secluded spot of memory. Kakati understood and accepted the inevitable. His wife was however a little confused. She was in a self explanatory believe that the day will be back that one day their children would return home after their studies. She awaited in the forlorn hope that her children would be living together with them. It was folly to be wise for her to remain blissfully ignorant.

Madhabi used to give company to Nilima for most of the time. When she laid down in her bed after her lunch for a short siesta Madhabi would come near her after finishing all her domestic chores in the kitchen. She would invariably bring the topic of the children. She was quite aware that such conversations were the most favourite topics for Nilima Kakati. She gave warm glowing smile and the conversation usually ran very ebulliently. In those moments her mind persistently remained in a state of reverie as though they were with her. Madhabi wanted to know many stories about the cities, their studies about their food and lodging. She had fantasized that the city was something unimaginably pleasing place like the havean because she did not have slightest idea of the both. Her questions were so basic that many a times Nilima found them ridiculous and preferred not to respond. Among the three children Madhabi had a special affinity to Nandita which was however not for the gender similarly. Nandita told her that she was studying human body and how human body functions. She sometime showed Madhabi the bones of human skeleton to scare her. She became fearful and all these knowledge failed to enter into her head. She could imagine people studying book but how could some one study human body? After death bodies were burnt at a deserted cremation ground near a river. The dead person's souls got transformed into nasty ghosts unless the rituals were performed. There were many ghosts of people who committed suicide or die an unnatural death. Those ghosts hide themselves under big banyan trees or bunch of bamboos and sometime in ponds. They stay in dark and forbidden places. People never visit those places and never discuss about ghosts in the night. The ghosts kill people or make them dumb or blind or make them mad. Her knowledge was limited to that extent and therefore she was frightened to look or to touch those human bones.

Quite unexpectedly Banibrata came home for a short stay for an urgent discussion with his parents. Presence of Banibrata to a great extent broke the loneliness and brought back life to the house. Apart from parents Madhabi became hyper active. Banibrata was a devoted family man. Whenever his was there he engaged himself in all sorts of duties like maintenance of house, compound etc.. He also worked in the vegetables garden. Banibrata replaced the old and worn out bamboo fencing around the compound by himself. In his young days Kakati used to do these work himself. He was expert in bamboo crafts. He used to make fans, sieve and fine colanders.

After hard labour Banibrata was exhausted and straight went to the tubewell to take bath. It was a bright sunny day. Then he entered father's room and sat near him. He looked thoughtful and he said in a very soft tone 'There is a semi town named Maniktola about three hundreds kilometre from here by road. The town is much bigger than ours. A degree college has been setup there by some leading residents nearly three years back. It had not received any govt. aid till now. The collage had sent an offer to me to join them as a lecturer. Hopefully the college would be taken up to by the govt. for financial aid shortly.'

Gobinda Kakati listened attentively. Suddenly his mind drifted to his own days when he started his career as a teacher in the school without remuneration at the venture stage. He remained silent and was pondering on the proposal.

Banibrata continued in a confident mood. 'Deuta, I feel that the offer is worthy of acceptance. I would like to get your opinion. People are expecting that government grants will not be delayed for long.'

'Offer is definitely good' A smile lifted the corner of his mouth. 'But its very far. When have they asked you to join?'

Banibrata shrugged and said 'They have not given any date. I think the immediately after completion of my final examination, I can join. Its true that the place is far from here, the journey is also quite tedious but the connectivity is not arduous. There is regular bus service from Guwahati and it takes about.' He rubbed his chin thoughtfully and said 'six to seven hours. But by train it's very clumsy.'

'How they will pay you?' He asked faintly with curiosity.

'Presently they will give me a minimal amount to meet my day today expenses. But after obtaining govt. grants regular pay will be given.'

Kakati smiled with relief and said 'I think it's a good proposal and you should accept the offer without hesitation.' However, you may think of coming to nearer place after words.' Kakati gave his consent in order to gratify his wishes.

Banibrata well understood the concern of his father. His parents are getting old, they obviously expect the children to be nearby. He perhaps hoped that one day a college may come up at Barsila even and then he could serve here. Banibrata became emotional and left his room and come to meet his mother. She was lying on the bed in the adjacent room. She had overheard the conversation faintly. She looked at Banibrata and asked adoringly 'What's upto Bani?' She rose and sat on the edge of the bed 'I heard something. That you are going some where?'

'Yes maa' He sat close to her and caressed his mother's hand and said 'I have got a job of lecturer in Maniktola College. It's about seven hours journey from here. Don't get panicked. I will come very frequently.' Unlike the school we get lot of time and break in college teaching job.'

She was pop eyed gave him a wary look and said 'Seven hours! Its almost a day. How do you go there?'

Banibrata consoled her and said 'Look maa, Maniktola is well connected from our place. Several buses ply from Guwahati. We have to change our bus at Guwahati. Now a days several modes of transport like bus, mini buses service are there. The distance hardly matters.'

Nilima Kakati knew above all else that her son must go. She rubbed her moisted eyes by the corner of her chaddar. Banibrata hold her both hands to cheer her up and stroked away her tears.

'Do not be sorrowful. I will keep coming to see you very often.'

Nilima Kakati tried to comfort herself and said falteringly. 'I know Bani, you will have to go.' She fought her tears and said we cannot keep you forever with us. You also can not waste your life only by staying at Barsila looking after us. You have to do something and build a career. But one thing pricked my heart very much'.

'What?' Banibrata eyed his mother with alarm.

Exhaling a deep breath she said 'You had to work from a very young age to supplement our family earnings. You have practically borne your educational expenses. I feel sad that you did not get rest from your young age. God knows everything. He will return you with full of blessings.' Actually there was extreme urgency for Banibrata to take up a job to support his siblings. Apart from his pay Gobinda Kakati had a little earnings from the agricultural income. He had sufficient agricultural land and some how managed the required money to maintain the family. With a little surplus he was partially meeting the educational expenses of

Nandita and Debabrata. Banibrata was a very considerate child, so he assured his father to share the financial burden on his shoulder. He could comprehend that gradually the entire burden would shift to him because Kakati was going to retire in next two years time.

'Alright maa, I will now go to the market. I will get the list of items from Madhabi, Take care.'

Nilima Kakati gave a sad smile. She then slowly got up from the bed and staggered to reach her small chest and turned the key to open the lock. She tookout some money and gave that to Banibrata. He initially thought to refuse but he thought that his refusal might hurt her sentiment and he took the money and went out. Banibrata called out Madhabi to come.

His mother lived all her years with a glimmer of hope that her son will come back home after completing their studies. All of a sudden a sense of despair flowed through out her body and she was dismayed. Warnings of imminent danger of desolation that they will face in future emerged in her mind. Among her children she had a self assurance that Banibrata was a sort of person they could depend on most. Nandita after graduation would take up job, would get married and would raise her own family. Nilima didn't have any crazy idea that her daughter could support them at their forlorn days. Her younger son took admission in IIT, Mumbai. She didn't have an iota of doubt he has already grown big and there will be no place to accommodate him at Barsila. She was certain that he would never comeback to stay at Barsila. Thus she had harboured remote possibility that Banibrata would one day come back to Barsila and would take up a job of teacher in the High School. She thought that teacher's job was befitting for him. She started believing that these were her wayward ambition driven by utter selfishness.

Since about last six months Madhabi was suffering from intermittent pain in her lower abdomen. Occasionally the pain became unbearably intense. She did not let anybody know about her discomfort. She was scared that her trouble might hamper the peace and tranquilly of the house. Her only purpose was that Mr. and Mrs. Kakati should not face any trouble because of her unfitness. So she tried to keep her sufferings under wraps from the family.

Madhabi was groaning due to acute pain in her abdomen at the time when Banibrat was calling her. She was unable to respond to Banibrata's call instantly. She staggered in stupor while walking. He looked at her frightfully. He guessed that she must be gravely ill, otherwise she never tottered like that.

'What happen to you? Are you sick?' Banibrata was stunned at the piteous site. She was almost groaning and said 'No, nothing to bother. As I ran my feet slipped and met with a fall.' She smiled falsely at her lie.

Banibrata could figure out that she was hiding something from him. His hand caressed the back of her neck and bowed his head and affably asked her 'I could see that you are suppressing your pain. I am sure you are suffering from some ailments. Be franks to me. I will consult a doctor for your treatment.'

She gave an uneasy look at Banibrata and told 'No, no, I am alright. Dada, please, do not make mountain out of a mole hill.' She rubbed her eyes with back of her hand.

Banibrata was convinced that the matter was far from normal. He thought that she might be suffering from some female disease. He admonished her told sternly 'Why did you not inform Maa or Nandita? Nandita could have given you some useful advice. By the way since how long you are feeling this pain?'

'Dada don't fuss everything, I am alright. I had some pain. It will disappear after some time. I have brought some local medicine from the old women there. She gave me an amulet.

Banibrata gave a defiant look and went out murmuring himself 'These people are never serious about their sickness. They depend more on miraculous power of healing.' People of Barsila till then believed that everything in life was fated and they perish with that faith. People had not developed the sense of trust in modern scientific health care facilities.

(4)

It is not death that a man should fear, but he should fear never beginning to live

- *Marcus Aurelius*

As the custom prevalent in those days marriage of girls started immediately after attainment of puberty. Madhabi had reached her marriageable age by then. Her father came to meet Gobinda Kakati in several occasions and persued him about her marriage. But Kakati was adamant and was not inclined to accept some poor and wretched farmer as suitor for Madhabi. He couldn't imagine to throw her in an appalling penury situation. Kakati's family was dreaming of getting her married with a suitable boy from Barsila town, who atleast had a job or a business who was able to maintain a family. Kakati assured Hari of their commitment for her. In fact Banibrata had identified a boy who had put up his shop recently in the town.

Nilima Kakati heard a sound of falling something behind her back. She was busy attending some work in the kitchen. She turned her attention towards the sound. She saw Madhabi fell on the floor. She looked wiped out due to pain. 'How did you fall?' Nilima Kakati tried to lift her and asked.

'I slipped over and fall down.'

She turned towards her and screamed 'what happen to you?' Nilima Kakati clearly saw her writhing around on the floor in agony and look at her queerily. 'What's the matter? Why you are crying?'

Madhabi struggled to hide her discomfort and she closed her eyes tightly.

Nilima yanked her to her feet and took her to bed. Madhabi staggered with her. She was a nervous wreck and rushed to her husband for advice.

Man proposes God disposes. Before the dream took a shape Madhabi was attacked by a dreaded ailment. She started feeling intermittent pain in her abdomen for past few months. Occurrence of her pain became more frequent and at times they were very intense. When consulted by Kakati the lone medical officer of Barsila gave her initial treatment. But all efforts were futile and there was no sign of recovery. Treatment at the local health centre was still in primitive state. The family plunged into deep anxiety, which continued till arrival of Nandita.

Nandita rushed home on receipt of the news. She took her to a room and tried to check the abdomen. She put her hand over the abdomen and pressed very slowly, very quietly and coaxingly as someone to a child to trace the exact location of the pain. She exclaimed 'it's a tumour!' She tried to feel the size more minutely and proceeded to untie the slip knot of her payjama. Madhabi was abashed and grabbed Nandita's hand. She was shy and reticent. Nandita scolded her and went ahead without paying any heed to her protest. Nandita was aghast that there was something seriously wrong with her.

She consulted the doctor at Barsila and discussed the matter with him. She then discussed the matter with her parents. Everybody resolved that Madhabi should be taken to Guwahati for better treatment. Nandita was too frightened to fore see the complexity of the problem. Her initial diagnosis was epitheliums of stomach.

Nandita went back to her college and she casually discussed the problem of Madhabi with her friends and her seniors. Nobody could confirm without physical investigation of the patient. So without further waste of time she had decided to bring Madhabi to Guwahati for thorough investigation and treatment. So Nandita came home again to fetch ailing Madhabi to Guwahati.

Madhabi was frightened when she was told than she would be taken to Guwahati for investigation and treatment. Her initial reaction was of shock and she vehimently raised a storm of protest and told "What will happen to Deuta and Aai? How can they stay alone. Its impossible for me to leave them."

After a series of admonition she finally succumbed and agreed to go to Guwahati. It had been a serious emotional upset to Nilima Kakati. She could not even say good bye to Madhabi. She could barely conceal her disappointment and she wiped tears from her eyes in seclusion.

Govinda Kakati's brother in law Rajat was a bank employee and resided in Guwahati permanently. Nandita and Madhabi proceeded to her maternal uncle's house who was already aware of their arrival. The climate was dry and windy. There was lot of dusts on the road all along the way. Immediately after getting down from the bus they stood and dusted themselves down. After reaching Rajat's house Nandita flung her bag in a bed and went straight to the wash room.

It was a pleasantly mild winter evening and the sun was behind the cloud. It was a holiday Rajat and wife were sitting in their living room and waited for Nandita. They looked with a curious tenseness as she entered the room. After the exchanging usual pleasantries they came to the main topic behind Madhabi. Nandita gave a brief idea of the symptoms of the disease, Madhabi was suffering. She expressed her anxiety running in the back of her mind. They were in sympathetic and thought of the possibilities.

Madhabi was put to several diagnostic tests in the medical college. Sample from the tumour was collected and sent for biopsy. Nandita had a feeling of heart throbbing moment when doctor suggested for a biopsy test. There was a great anxiety for all. They had stern disbelief that young Madhabi might suffer from any dreaded disease.

After a week of emotional upheaval the final report of biopsy reached, the doctor called Nandita and he pronounced his confirmation.

'It's positive' Doctor was apparently sad but composed. His voice was level and cautions. 'She is suffering from malignant tumour. This type of malignancy do not show much of symptoms early. But they grew fairly large before detection and progressively worsen the condition.'

Nandita was stunned with fright. She had lost the last gleam of hope and shook her head in disbelief. As she heard the words from the doctor her eyes filled with tears. She started to sob and she muttered in quavering voice. 'Sir, what is the treatment? How is the condition? Is it in a stage for treatment?'

'Peritoneal cancer can be treated with surgical intervention which could have been tried at initial stage. But in her case the carcinomas cells might have already spread to other parts of the body. Now treatment will be very long and expensive. Over and above continuous long term nursing and follow up will be extremely important. However chances of recovery looks very bleak.'

'What should we do then Sir?' Nandita could not hold back her emotion. She was sobbing and said in unsteady voice'Kindly suggest some solutions Sir.'

'I understand your worry. You can go for radiation therapy or a sort of palliative therapy for relief. Surgery and chemo therapy will be very expensive and I personally like to rule out those in her case. If you allow me to be frank all these efforts are likely to be a futile exercise.'

Rajat tried to console Nandita to calm down. She dipped her head on the chest of her uncle. They slowly came out from the doctor's chamber and went straight to Rajat's house.

None of them could gather courage to face Madhabi. But strangely enough she was in her usual discourse. She was with Rajat's wife in the Kitchen arranging lunch for them. She was not in any uneasiness. Nandita repeatedly told her to take rest. But rest was perhaps not there in her dictionary. From the day one she entered Kakati's family she was on the go, she was unstoppable. She had identified herself heart and soul with that family and perhaps forgot her real identify.

All of them sat quietly in the sitting room of Rajat's house. They confided about the next course of action. Should they go for further treatment which obviously they could not afford and also was uncertain of any positive result. Should they send her back to the family at the village which sounded immoral? What should they do?

Rajat finally said 'I think' he rubbed his forehead and bunched his eyebrow 'It will not be feasible to go for extensive treatment. Financial back up will be inadequate. Even if we picture that in our mind who will provide her nursing. Constant nursing will be required during and after her treatment. We do not have any man power for nursing. Above all as the doctor opined that all efforts are likely to be futile.'

Nandita shook her head in disapproval. 'You mean, we just don't go for any treatment and send her home at this stage? These is no facilities for any treatment in the village. She will have to sadly wait for a painful death.' Nandita envisoned the awful atmosphere in her parental house. They were extremely impoverished people and instead of taking her care they will urge for her early death and get relief. Not to speak of medicine, even food will be scarce.' She again said 'Who will attend and administerthe midicines? Where they would get medicines. Only dispensary at Barsila town was about three kilometres away from their house. That dispensary was also no better than a first aid centre with some tincture and quinine'. Tears gathered in her eyes.

Rajat raised his both hands and tried to convince Nandita 'Let's call spade a spade. We must accept the reality. I sympathise her for misfortune. We are now in such a precarious situation that there is no option before us, We have to accept God's will with grace. Your mother is also incapacitated due to her general weakness. Truely speaking she is unfit to take care of herself and for her to attend such a patient is out of question. So Nandita you may suggest some pain killers to alleviate her sufferings and discomfort within reach.'

'Agreed, till her end?' Nandita gave a little twist to her head and said in a murmurous voice. 'But its not easy to tell her that. She will vehemently refuse to go.' She had a puzzled look on her face. She thought 'how cruel it will be to discard her like an old donkey who became too weak to work. To throw the bottle of perfume once the smell is finished.

At night Nandita asked Madhabi to come to her room to sleep over to empathize with her. She could not reconcile herself with the inevitable consequence of losing her. Madhabi was lying on the floor near her bed. 'Madhabi' Nandita called Madhabi is a quavering voice with opposite intentions of charming up. 'Don't get panicked. Your disease is curable. Doctors have given some medicines, I will also give you. With regular use of the medicines tumour will shrink and you will be cured. Sleep now.'

Nandita's encouraging words soothed her and her spirit soared high.

'What a relief' Madhabi said with a cheerful voice. 'I know its not a dreaded disease. I will be alright. All of you have made a big issue.'

There was an unusual calmness in the room. Nandita broke down and was silently sheding tears.

Next day Nandita took Madhabi back their home.

After getting the news, Govinda Kakati was horrified and his face was drained of colours. He was nervous as he encountered with an incomprehensible problem. In his long life he had not come across with such a struggling situation other than occasional financial hardship. He shook his head looked up and whispered 'What a deadly blow you have given my lord? Why such a young girl is punished mercilessly, much before she could see the life?'

Govinda Kakati had a very tough time to pass on the news to his wife. Nilima was shocked and wailed in disbelief. Nandita came running to her and tried to pacify her so that Madhabi's spirit did not go down and cause an adverse affect. It was strange sight that Madhabi was not at all bothered about the gravity of her ailment She trusted what Nandita told her the previous night and was certain of her recovery. Ironically it was Madhabi who tried to console Nilima Kakati

'Our Nanditaba baideo has assured me that the tumour will be gradually reduced in size and finally disappear. I will recover shortly. Please do not take unnecessary tension.'

Nilima Kakati was sobbing uncontrollably and was extremely tired and exhausted. Madhabi wrapped her arms around her waist. She led her to the bed. Nilima Kakati was whimpering and desperately trying to fight back the tears.

After series of discussion between Nandita and her father they reached a consensus decision to sent Madhabi back to her home. In fact there was no alternative but to accept the practical aspect of situation. They decided to send an intimation to Hari accordingly.

Gobinda Kakati was crest fallen and confused, how to tell Madhabi that they had decided to send her back to her village. Everybody has a dream to live happily in this world with hope and aspirations. She was quite young to have many such dreams in her heart. But destiny had some other plan for her. Kakati was certain that she would never agree to go back to her village. She will vehemently protest and beg him not to send her. His mind was in terrible vexation. He could not pluck up the courage to tell her the truth. At last after a few days Govinda Kakati called Madhabi and looked at her with mystification. He did not look to her eyes and told that it would be wise for her to go back home and wait for recovery so that she could take nest and regain her strength.

The moment Madhabi heard those words from Kakati she became hysterical. She was vehemently protesting with pititul wailing and whined 'No, No deuta, Please. I pray you be mereyful. Please do not send me back, don't send me, I wont go. I will die here.'

That was a pitiful scene. At one time she stopped and dispersed from there. Kakati stood motionless in the same place, gazing the open sky with pensive mood. His eyes were filled with tears which he did not like to frought back.

It was a dull dizzy morning. Kakati got up with the sun. He woke every morning at the same time. After a brief stroll in the compound, he sat on the chair at the outside courtyard. Sun was gradually up in the sky in full humid heat. He looked up to sky blankly, a mood of melancholy descended on him. Banibrata was in home. He joined his father and sadly sat in an adjacent chair.

There was a sound of some one opening their bamboo gate. Both Kakati and Banibrata turned their heads towards the sound. Hari with another unknown person entered slowly and came near Kakati. Hari and his companion touched Kakati's feet and stood calmly. After a little general talk Kakati straight way said in a grave voice. 'Madhabi is suffering from a serious disease. She was examined by reputed doctors at Guwahati. The disease is a rare one and is very critical.'

The news hit them like a thunderbolt. Hari was dumb founded and close to tears. He could not imagine even in the wildest dream of such a misfortune. They dropped and sat near Kakati and awaited speechlessly. Even if he had or wanted to say something, he could not utter as the words got stuck in his throat.

After sometime Kakati indicated Banibrata to bring Madhabi. Nilima Kakati already prepared her for her deparature. She put her hand on the back of her neck. Both were in extreme sadness. Madhabi broke into tears and could not contain her emotions when she approached and bent to touch Kakati's feet to beg leave of him. She wept bitter tears could not hide her emotions. Kakati kept his right hand over her head. Kakati had a dream to bid her farewell on her marriage. He would have wept for joy. But what a paradox of the situation? He had to say good bye to her for ever with a heavy heart. Tears gathered in his eyes.

'Madhabi' Kakati walked with her in slow pace and said in a shaking voice 'don't exhert yourself much. Take rest. Take the medicines, regularly. Keep trust upon God.' After a pause he gathered all strength to pronounce those terrible words. 'Take the medicines regularly, the tumour will slowly shrink and then you come here again and after treatment in Guwahati you will be fully cured.'

Both Madhabi and Kakati couldn't look at each other. Both were gazing below and the air of false hope swayed both. The whole story was nothing but a pack of lies.

Madhabi left the house with Hari for good. Kakati didn't believe how could he tell such a naked lie. Specially when he never took refuse to such a falsehood in his long life. He sat for quite a long just gazing into the space. Tears welled up in his eyes and rolled down his cheek. Tears are the silent language of grief. He prayed for forgiveness from God. He hoped that God will be merciful and absolve him of the sin he had to commit under compulsion.

(5)

Human behaviour flows from three main sources, desire, emotion and knowledge

-   Plato

Swaraswati the goddess of learning was worshipped in the medical college with much grandeur like all other educational institutions. Apart from seeking blessings from the goddess of learning the students took it as a great occasion for diversion from monotonous studies and enjoyed it as an annual celebration. The girl students all over the city irrespective of age attired themselves with elegant traditional dresses. This was an occasion for a grand get together of friends from different institutions. Young boys took advantage of Swaraswati puja celebration as a good opportunity of meeting their female friends though most of them had to satiate themselves by catching a glimpse of the charming girls in the crowd. Many students try to talk to the girls in vain. Some lucid as well as disastrous stories also happened on the occasion.

Dipen Das a class mate of Nandita bore an indomitable urge to earn intimacy with her since the day they became group mate in their practical anatomy classes. He had a strong belief that the students of medical college should select a girl friend and marry her in due course. He was guided by that conventional notion and he yearn to make a relationship with Nandita, as the first step towards his goal in his mind. Nandita was a warm and friendly girl, for which she was very popular among her friends. She had a pretty good look. She including her friends were well aware of the earnest desire of Dipen to secure intimacy.

In the late evening. Nandita was chatting with her friends at a corner of the puja premise in a lighter jovial mood. Only a few girls were there while many of them had left for city. The boy's hostel was almost deserted as all the boarders have gone to visit different colleges to watch the geity and glamour of the celebration and to take glance of devoted pretty girls. Dipen was the lonely exception. He refused to go with his hostel mates under some false excuses. His heart and soul was in the college premise where Nandita was there. He was a staunch believer of the old saying 'one in hand is better that two in the tree.'

It was dark outside because in winter the sun sets early. Dipen put on a sweater and came out to look for Nandita in the college puja premise. He advanced to the group of girls where Nandita was chuckling and chatting. Seeing Dipen looming towards them the girls abruptly stopped. Dipen looked fairly embarrassed at their bizarre reaction. The girls could not hide their amusement at the way he was standing before them. One of the girls asked him 'Dipen what's upto? You didn't go out to visit the alluring pageants waiting in the puja stalls of colleges in the city? The pretty girls in attractive dresses were all waiting like participants in a beauty contest.'

Dipen gasped and smiled foolishly. He was confused how to respond. He felt a warm blush rise to his cheeks. The another girls told with a bantering tone in her voice 'Why do you feel so shy to express yourself. Actually you want to be exclusively with Nandita? Am I right?' The girls chortled with delight and went aside.

Dipen fumbled helplessly and shook his head. He gathered strength to tell 'Yes, I want to spend some time with her.'

Nandita also had a bit of soft corner for him and she came to his rescue. 'Yes you should say that openly. What's the harm, we are classmates and we can be friendly.'

Nandita tried to create an atmosphere of warmth and geniality and politely said 'Dipen, meek people are usually bullied by others. Now a days politeness is largely considered as weakness.'

Dipen smiled encouragingly. 'But I always try to keep away from girls. I don't feel ease with them even if they are my classmates.'

Nandita laughed 'You are crazy.'

'But I enjoy your company. I want to be intimate with you.' He said.

Nandita appreciated the frankness of Dipen. She believed that feelings for some one should be expressed without duplicity. If you want to say no, say no at the first instant but she could not say no.

'Nandita' Dipen said with a smile 'Thanks for a great evening, I really enjoyed it.'

That was their first one to one contact and slowly their relations turned to an affair. Dipen was a very bright student and always secured top position in the class. So there was a tendency for his class mates to become close to him for their selfish interest. Dipen was a credulous boy and he was always eager to help whoever approached him. Obviously Nandita was the one who was benefitted most from Dipen. He used to guide her and cleared all her confusion in studies.

Nandita hailed from an old fashioned middle class family with a rural background. She was a complete novice in the city surrounding and she had a bit of hurdle to make herself accustomed to the new situation. Due to the sudden change in situation she was to some extent swayed away by the pomposity of the city life.

It was solely for Dipen that she could make it through in college examination. He was very serious and made all efforts to make Nandita attentive in studies and successfully pass out in the examination. Nandita enticed Dipen for watching movies. Then to go to restaurant, to go for shopping which he had to accept unwillingly. Eventually the news of their love affairs reach students ear. There were however diversed opinion about the sustainability of their relations because many of them considered Nandita's affinity as a frivolous past time, because she was known for her easy manner.

The news of the love affairs between Dipen and Nandita also reached Banibrata who in turn passed on the same to their maternal uncle Rajat, who was also her local guardian. Both were in confusion and were apprehensive about her on going studies. They were not aversed to her love affairs but their concern was that the affair should not create more harm than help. They debated on the matter and wished her promising career at the same time they were highly sceptical that any adversity would damage the reputation of the whole family of Gobinda Kakati.

After a couple of days Nandita came to her uncle's place to spend a week end holiday. She felt refreshed in their home from the monotonous hostel life because of their warmth and delicious food. Rajat's wife was a kind and homely woman. She always spoke in colloquial language as spoken by the rural people of lower Assam and Nandita relished talking to her. She was older than Nandita by a few years but they were very friendly and discussed anything under the sun openly. Chatting with her was a great recreation for Nandita because, she felt suffocating to be continuously buried herself in those tasteless books and the envious girls, whom she called classmates.

Rajat's wife already got the sensuous news of Nandita's affair with one of her classmates before hand. She got in a flap in slightest things, so she was very much excited and was eagerly awaiting for meeting Nandita at the earliest. Rajat talked with Nandita a few general things over the breakfast and then he left for office in a hurry. He did not raise the topic of her affairs because he knew very well that his wife would surely descuss the fascinating story in details.

After finishing all morning domestic chores Rajat's wife called Nandita to the living room for the purpose of a long chatt. She straight away came to the most curious subject. She was ofcourse not certain how important the topic was for Nandita or how serious she was in the matter. Because she was aware of the insouciant behaviour of Nandita.

Both of them eased themselves in the sofa and readied for the cozy chat. Rajat's wife threw her hairs back and initiated 'So Nandita how is everything going with you?' She gave an amusing glance at Nandita.

'Mami', She twisted her lips 'It's fine. But day by day I am finding the study materials tough and to be frank more boring.'

'Why didn't you take help from some friends who are studious?' She dropped a wicked hint.

Nandita nodded her head 'Yes, I have to' She suddenly waggled in her seat. 'I have a very close friend, Dipen Das. He is a local boy and we are classmates. He is a very polite and innocent boy and a real book worm.' She chuckled.

Rajat's wife could not control her delight and gave a gleeful laugh 'We know! We know that you are having an affair with him. I am actually glad to get the news confirmed from the horses mouth.'

Nandita looked with popeyed and gave a bemused smile. She could not imagine that the news of her premature affairs got so much publicity. She glanced cursorily and said 'Mami, I am not sure what you have in your store. At the moment we are close friends. He helped me a lot.' She tittered 'He is bent upon to make me pass the exam at ease.'

Curiosity arosed in her mind and she gazed at Nandita in amazement.

Nandita again said 'Dipen is topper in our class. So I have taken full advantage of him. His courtly love is from the core of his heart. I could make out.'

Rajat wife quipped 'He must be good doctor in future. So don't let him loose. Hold him tight.' She chortled wrinking at her. 'Why don't you take him to our place.' Rajat's wife said in a soft and cajoling voice 'We will have long chatt and will have chance to know each other.'

Nandita hinted a smile and said 'He is very shy and not very comfortable with new people, specially with opposite sex. That is his prosaic side of life.'

Rajat's wife giggled and said 'He will perhaps faint when he hear my outrageous colloquial language.' The room roared with laughter.

'Hope he will enjoy you oddities of language.' Nandita retorted back.

The conversation then turned to other topics around Barsila, Moment the name of Barsila appeared both became gloomy and silent. Nandita was in sorrowful eyes. There was a deafening silence. They prayed God for the eternal peace of her soul.

'Mami' Nandita said in a low voice 'I still suffer from a guilty conscience as if we have not done proper justice to her.' She served us to her best selflessly, And what we have given her in return.

'Nandita' Rajats wife shrugged her shoulder and said 'What can you do? We are nobody against the will of the God.' She stood up and walked towards kitchen 'Let us cook some food now.'

Both went inside the kitchen. 'Mami', Nandita said in a grave tone 'Some time I feel deep pain inside my heart when I visualise the remorseful future of my parents at Barsila. How they will pass their time? How they will manage to take care of each other? We could not do anything, for anybody in life in true sense. We live for ourselves.'

'Nandita these are the most complex matters in life specially faced by people in their fag end. Nobody can do anything. Forget about the future. Live in the present.'

(6)

Pride goeth before destraction and an haughty spirit before a fall

- ***Bible***

Prasanta Barua a former a senior engineer in state government had an unobliterate fascination for his native place Maniktola. He served in several places throughout Assam and gathered multifarious experiences both bitter and better. Unlike many others he had no crave for settling in Guwahati. For him the city life is suffocating and that was not his cup of tea. Barua had grown very attached to his semi developed home town. Where he felt a deep affinity with nature. All put together the alluring pull of his town haunted him throughout his life. He had an ancestral house in the heart of the town. Within a reasonable expenses the house was renovated. A few leading citizens with visionary zeal had set up a college at Maniktola a few years back. Necessity of an institution of higher education was long felt. Barua's only child Malabika joined very recently as a lecturer in English department in that college. So that became an additional consideration for him to settle in Maniktola.

Mrs. Barua however was unhappy with the decision of her husband for settling at Maniktola. She objected to her husband's ridiculous idea. The town lacked all modern amenities including adequate proper health care facilities. There was no place of entertainment. She even did not like her daughter Mala to join the newly established college in the town. She believed that her daughter should not waste time in such a sluggish place which had no future. All her potentials, her aspirations, her talent would be lost and she would be suffering from severe boredom and glumness.

Mrs. Barua had every reason to be proud of her daughter. Malabika was so charming that even a nymph would be put to shame. Apart from her unrivalled beauty she was also front runner in the academics and cultural fields. She used to fetch prizes in sports in her young age. She was the first girl student to obtain a masters degree from the town and for that matter in the surrounding locality. All residents specially the girls irrespective of age of those area knew her as a role model.

Prasanta Barua was a obstinate man. The rule with his wife was never to provoke him and therefore she compromised with the decision of her husband to settle at Maniktola permanently for the shake of domestic peace. In the small town like Maniktola the women regularly paid visit to the public prayer house (Namghar). There during the gap period of reciting religious verses, the devotees normally engaged themselves in idle gossip. Mrs. Barua was a regular visitor to the Naamghar. In course of those gassips occasionally the issue of Malabika's marriage emerged with curiosity among them though those were just superficial concern for most of them. Far from being annoyed she savoured the topic with obvious relish.

Without any sign of hesitation Mrs. Barua would boastfully say 'I can't believe that there is any suitable suitor for her in Maniktola and I doubt whether there is any in Guwahati. He must be in America.'

Her friends tried to dampen her spirituous remarks 'She is your only child. How will you stay here alone if you send her abroad? She will not be able to come here every now and then. You will miss her at your old age. She will not be near you when you are in fraught with difficulties.'

She looked visibly annoyed. Her eyes glinted angrily and said in a sardonic atone. 'If I need her very often than I will have to keep her in my house as spinster and waste all her God gifted charm. Don't worry we have a plan for her.'

Her friends used to talk behind her back and ventilate their displeasure. Malabika was no doubt exceptionally pretty and virtuous but they did not appreciate the haughty swanks of her mother. Singing her vain glory might end up in grave peril. One of them said 'Pride goes before a fall.'

Actually there was some inkling in her mind because of the fact that there was a proposal from a boy who dwelt in America. A very premature link appeared a few days ago. Prasanta Barua's younger brother Robin was a permanent resident of New Jersey in USA. He was a green card holder citizen of that country. He mulled a proposal for Mala for a boy from Assam who was staying in New Jersey and serving in a reputed multinational company in information technology sector. His name was Pradyut Phukan. According to Robin, Pradyut had a good family back ground. He was ofcourse not sure of his character in literal sense of word. In those societies normally people do not discuss those private affairs opnely. They call it respect to the private life.'

Robin also mentioned that Pradyut's father was a senior administrative civil servant in the state government. But there was a delicate problem in the proposal. Phukans were from Ahom community.

Robin finally left the decision to the prudence of his elder brother Prasanta Barua to take the proposal forward. 'I have expressed my views as per I conceived. The rest is yours to decide. If you find it acceptable then you let me know.'

At first sight the proposal appeared to be very attractive. Nothing could be perhaps better than that. The most attractive point was that the boy stayed in the states and he is serving in a reputed company. Malabika would be delighted to accept it. The matter of caste barrier however was of concern. The age old tradition and customs were not easy to disown so easily. That was still a taboo in the society. Violations of the norms were visible only in rare cases of marriage consummated after love affairs. But in case of arranged marriage intercaste marriages were not widely prevelant in the society.

Barua walked into the kitchen with a mixed feeling of cheerfulness in one hand and censorious feeling on the other. He said to himself 'Fortune comes but with a cost.' He ran inside to pass on the news to his wife.

'Robin has sent a tempting proposal for our Mala. Amazing. The boy stays in America. It just fitted to your dream.' Barua said with a smile wreathed in his face.

His wife caught a gleamer in her eyes. She rubbed her hands in her chadar and looked at him quizzically and said 'Tell me quickly the details. What he had written? Let me put off the gas.'

Barua smiled exultantly and started reading the letter loudly. At the half way of reading both said grace for such a blessing to them. Before coming out from the kitchen Barua read the last para of the letter and turned back and mildly made a cursory comment about the caste and community of Pradyut. 'The matter of caste is a little hitch and needs delicate handling. We live in a society, among our relatives. We simply can not deny the existence of the society.'

'What do you mean?' Mrs. Barua pounded her feet and gave a sneering comment. 'Forget your society, relatives, what they have done to you? Tell me how many of your friends and relatives want our happiness by heart. Please stop these nonsense and work on the proposal without delay. Don't forget that delayed reaction in these matters spoil the chances. I am not going to be silenced by the society. I will never allow this proposal to go in vain. This proposal should not go out of our hand at any cost.'

'Wait, wait' Barua raised his hand and gestured his wife to remain calm and said 'There may be another probability. Robin has told that he is not sure of his character. We have to carefully look into that part also. It's a matter of life for Mala. She is our only child.'

'Look' Mrs. Barua's face foisted in anger and said in a taunting voice 'You have already started with a negativity. Evil thoughts already started sprouting in your mind. Are you aware that your daughter has already crossed her marriageable age?' She then murmured 'At her age Mala was five years old. Fathers are simply soulless.' She left Barua in dejection.

Prasanta Barua restrained his feelings and said sardonically. 'All that glitters are not gold.'

Prasanta Barua gave a placating smile and touched gently on her arm and said in a whispering tone 'You discuss the proposal with Mala. She is a matured and educated girl. Her mind is also a very important. She must gladly accept it. After all it is she who has to be happy.'

Mrs. Barua said with confidence. 'I don't think she will have any objection. She is intelligent enough to visualise future happiness in life. She can't afford to discard this proposal. She is educated enough not to bother about the caste.'

Barua intercepted 'Still there is a gap between the cap and the lip.'

Mrs. Barua shook her head in disapproval of the sarcastic comment of her husband and said 'We have raised her with all humane virtues. She is jem of a girl. She has a cultured mind and defiance of our decision is most improbable. Moreover we have not picked up an unworthy chap from Maniktola for her. He is from America, the land of affluence. She will be able to muster all happiness and comfort of life. What more she will yearn for?'

Barua was looking at his wife and patted on her back. He said in a low voice 'You have started dreaming as if the marriage is already accomplished. My belief is that we should never become over confident.

There is some force guiding us – call it God, destiny or fate. It was only by the grace of God everything moves on this universe. We are puppets only.'

Barua went out towards the town. His mind was working in a blistering pace. His intention was to confide with his best friend, who was his colleague and now settled in Guwahati and wanted to gather some information about Parbati Kumar Phukan and his son Pradyut as well from him.

Malabika came home in the afternoon. Dark clouds suddenly appeared in the sky and the whole of Maniktola got plunged into mild darkness. Mrs. Barua forgot that she made tea for her husband and the same was left untouched. She walked hastily to the kitchen. Tea was cold and spoiled. She threw those and started to make tea for Mala and herself. Mala shouted from her room. 'Maa I don't need tea now. I am tired and I will take some rest.'

'Thats fine dear' Her mother agreed. She had lost her desire for a cup of tea. She quietly came to her room and flang herself to the bed. She earnestly prayed 'Oh My God, what a blessing.

(7)

Let us always meet each other with smile, for the smile is the beginning of love

- *Mother Teresa*

The students of the Medical College made a plan to stage a play on the day of valediction as a part of celebration of their college week. They had selected one of the most famous plays of Shakespeare 'Julius Caesar'. The reason behind the selection of that drama was because the plot had mostly male characters. The girl students didn't show much interest in the proposal. Therefore the students decided that they will select a drama where there will be little presence of female artist. Among the students Anjan was the most capable and enthusiastic. He reserved the role of Antonius for himself and in addition he took the responsibility of direction. Anjan spotted Nandita, a jovial and frank girl two year junior to him for the role of Caesar's wife.

One day Anjan met Nandita in the canteen and revealed their plan of performing the theatre. He requested Nandita to take part in the drama and her instant reaction was steely rejection because Nandita was completely unfamiliar with acting. Anjan had a great power of persuation and she finally consented to the proposal. She was offered the role of Calphurnia, wife of Julius Caesar. Anjan requested Nandita to regularly attend the rehearsal sessions. Anjan had such a strength of personality that she did not dare to disobey him. He was very serious of the punctuality of all actors without exception. Nandita loved the way Anjan was teaching her how to deliver dialogues and move the body for perfect portrayal of the real character.

Dipen was opposed to the proposal of taking part in drama to be staged in the college as a part of celebration of college week. Dipen learnt that Nandita was taking part in the drama. He met her after the class hour.

'Nandita' Dipen looked very grave 'I have come to know that you are taking part in the drama. I am not happy with your decision.'

Nandita quipped 'Why? What's wrong in that?'

'I don't know I dislike such show business. I have an abhorrence to the glamorous world.' He told shaking his head.

Nandita did not say anything. There was an awkward silence. Dipen was surprised to see where from he gathered so much courage to stand against Nandita? He pondered.

'Dipen' Nandita broke silence and said in an intent tone 'It's a fun. It's a college function. I am not going for acting outside. Why should you have objection for it? It sounds quite silly.'

'No its not silly.' Dipen turned his head away 'Look you will have to spend hours in rehearsals with all those boys whom you do not know well. Is it not a waste of time which could be otherwise utilized for fruitful purpose. This may hamper your studies.'

'Studies, studies and studies' Nandita said furiously 'Damnit. One cannot be absorbed all the time in studies. People need relaxation, a break from monotonous work. How can you be so bird brained?'

Dipen looked at her face with disapproval. 'We have joined this college to study with the aim of becoming a good doctor. Obviously fun and relaxation are nothing but detraction and we should not be swayed by all these.'

Nandita looked at him with startled eyes. She was becoming increasingly stubborn and wanted to leave the place without passing any remark. She didn't like to externed the arguments further. She just went away from the place and left for her hostel. She was disgusted at the irrational behaviour of Dipen. She was disgusted to see that Dipen could be so mean and sceptical. The acting was just an entertainment, a fun of college days. What was there to be scornful about that? Did he suspect her fidelity for which he had no authority till then. Had he no confidence on her? His malicious mind made her blood boil. She was bewildered how can a relationship sustain under a cloud of mistrust. A wave of nausea swept over her.

Nandita didn't go out from her hostel next day and abstained from attending classes and her rehearsals. She looked so dejected that her roommates also hesitated to talk to her. After elapse of one full day her roommates enquired her to find out what was wrong with her. Water welled up in her eyes. After a respite she explained the conflict, she had with Dipen in connection with her taking part in the college drama. Her friends were astounded by the mindless arrogance of Dipen.

After much persuasion finally Nandita resumed her classes as usual. She regained her normalcy. Dipen glanced at her contritely and refrained from talking to her. He was suffering from a sense of guilt. Next day he came near Nandita and said in acquiescent tone. 'Nandita, I know you are enraged with me.' He dropped his head 'But I stand to whatever I said. Once mind gets engaged in such type of activities the main focus gets lost.'

'Dipen' Nandita said firmly 'I could manage my worries myself. You better concentrate in your affairs. I have decided to live my own life.'

Dipen was not prepared for such a shocking jolt. Words failed him. He stood motionless and looked her fixedly, as if the girl standing by his side was unknown to him. He was convinced that Nandita had not forgiven him and the matter went beyond reproach. He visualised that a lifeless replica of Nandita was standing near him. He heard Nandita slowly walked away from him. He desperately fought back the tears and stormed off.

Dipen was dejected that Nandita had treated him like that. He cautioned her for her own good but such a reaction could evoke was beyond his imagination. 'Was their relationship so fragile that it could end up abruptly and that too in such a flimsy conflict'. She would not have lost anything had she refused to act on the play.' He thought. But at the same time haven would not have fallen for Dipen when Nandita took part in the play. Dipen was sad that all his dreams with Nandita suddenly shattered before it could take a definite shape.

After a series of rehearsals the penultimate day of the occasion came. The college auditorium was packed to capacity with teachers, students and other employees of the college. The students have made every effort to decorate the stage as a true replica of the court of Caeser. The big back screen had been decorated with a broken pillars representing the Forum of Rome the court of Caesar. The drama progressed and the audience encouraged the actors by frequent applause. Moment the play reached its chimax the audience were in rapt attention. Julius Caesar entered the stage, followed by his wife Calplurnia (Nandita). On the previous might she dreamt a dream that some people killed Caeser. She solicited Ceasar not to go to the court. She begged Caeser 'You shall not stir out of your house today.' Caesar retorted 'Caesar shall forth, the things that threatened me, never looked but on my back, when they shall see, the face of Caesar they are vanished.' Caesar pushed his wife and boastfully said 'What can be avoided, whose end in purposed by the mighty God. Cowards die many times before their death the valiant never taste death but once. Seeing that death, a necessary end, will come when it will come.'

Caeser again said with self praise 'Danger knows full well that Caeser is more dangerous than he. We were two lions littered in one day and I am the elder and more terrible and Caeser shall go forth.'

Then he walked to the court followed by the senators. In the court room the nobles got in heated arguments with Caeser. At one time

Casca suddenly stabbed Caeser at his neck from behind. There was noisy scuffle in the stage Caeser fall down and finally his closest friend Brutus approached and stabbed him. Caeser was lying on the floor in the pool of blood. Finally he groaned 'Et to Btute!'

Brutus addressed the gathering to pacify them and to justify his action 'Romans country men and lovers! hear me for my cause; and be silent, that you may hear. Have respect to mine honour and awake your sense that you may better judge. If there be any in this assembly any dear friend of Caesar's, to him I say that Brutu's love to Caesar was no less than his. If then that friend demand, why Brutu's rose against Caesar, this is my answer - Not that I loved Caesar less, but that I loved Rome more.'

The audience cheered in appreciation of the performance of the actor.

At that moment Marcus Antonius (Anjan) stamped into the stage. There was total silence and all eyes were on him. He delivered the dialogue in sonorous voice shook with emotion. There was no humming sound in the auditorium. Emotions running high among the people of Rome.

Antony delivered his dialogues 'Friends, Romans, country men lend me your ears.

'I come to bury Caesar not to praise him. The evil that men do lives after them. The good is oft interned with their bones. So let it be with Caesar. The noble Brutus hath told you, Caesar was ambitious. If so it was a grievous fault. And grievously hath Caesar answered it. He hath brought many captives home to Rome. Whose ransoms did the general coffers fill. Did this in Caesar seem ambitious? When that the poor have cried, Caesar hath wept. Ambition should be made of sterner stuff. Yet Brutus says, he was ambitions and Brutus is an honourable man.' Anjan delivered his dialogue eloquently and he did not have to depend upon the prompter. Anjan was in fall command of his cast. He modulated his voice flawlessly and the dialogues and the audience was overcome with emotions. After few more dialogues he delivered his final speech was 'If you have tears, prepare to shed them now. This was the noblest Roman of them all. He, only, in a general honest thought and common good to all, made one of them. His life was gentle and the elements so mixed in him, that nature might stand up and say to all the world. This was a man.'

The moment Anjan wrapped up his dialogue the audience broke into rapturous applause, which resonated in the auditorium for quite some time. At the end when all the actors lined up on the stage the audience rose to applaud the actors for their enthralling performances.

Anjan is immaculate performance deeply impressed Nandita. Over and above Anjan was aptly charming. During all the rehearsal seasons Nandita had noticed a gracefully attractive look in his eyes. Nandita was highly charmed by the courteous nature of Anjan and slowly she developed a liking for him. The students who participated in the drama decided to celebrate their successful performance with a treat. Accordingly a programme for a dinner was set and participants were invited to join the dinner party with their contributions arranged in a nearby restaurant. Incidentally Nandita was the lone girl and she dithered to take decision to join the party which might run to late night. Moreover in such types of party the boys arrange hard drinks, which Nandita might not relish.

After series of persuasion Nandita agreed to attend with a condition that she will take a friend with her. Everybody agreed that instead of monetory contribution she will bring a guest. Boys didn't object rather they felt cheered that one more girl will join them. The deal was like buy one and get one free.

Anjan actually personally requested Nandita to come because he already developed a soft spot for her. He took his seat by the side of

Nandita and politely said 'Thank you for joining us. I was worried that your absence would have left our party incomplete.'

Nandita was blushed in romantic tickle and remained quiet. She found Anjan quite different from the rest. While a few of the boys were chatting in high pitched tone Anjan had occasional flashes of silence that made conversation more delightful. The boys were enjoying their drinks sitting at a corner. Nandita and her friend felt a bit awkward. However a sense of security prevailed upon them because of Anjan's presence by their side. Anjan was also slowly drinking. One of the boys approached Nandita and her friend and cajoled to taste the beer. After repeated persuasion Nandita slowly sipped the beer and she instantly grimaced at the bitter taste. The boys enjoyed the reaction and laughed. Anjan chided them for their crude joke. Finally the party came to an end. Everybody enjoyed the evening. The boys thanked the girls and begged perdon for their playful jest. Girls responded with cheerful smile.

Day by day Anjan and Nandita came closer and their friendship grew to deep intimacy. They met in canteen everyday almost at same time to have their morning tea and somosa. Hot somosa was most favourite of Anjan. Nandita was equally passionate to meet Anjan as well as to enjoy tea with him.

In the mean time they had started going out to city restaurants and to the river bank parks etc. from the college in the evening to spend some exclusive time. Nandita never ever imagined that one day she will be caught red handed in such a peculiar situation. She went to zoo with Anjan on a sunny winter day. During the winter season large number of visitors come to the zoo to watch the animals from close range. Some visitors of course come inside with their girl friends to intimately sit in some serene corners under the tall tree. Obviously the traffic in front of the zoo in those days became a headache for the police. The vehicles were allowed to pass intermittently to allow safe crossing of people. Rajat was waiting in his scooter at the traffic signal. Nandita and Anjan also reached that spot on their way back at that particular time. Both unexpectedly appeared just in front of him. Nandita was visibly baffled. She smiled nervously at his steady gaze. She was dithering about what to say 'What are you doing here uncle? Are going some where?' She gushed without much thinking because it was she who was supposed to give an explanation and not Rajat to do. Actually she tried to hide herself from a guilty feeling. Nandita again said in a quick accent 'We were looking for some break from the everyday mundane matters. So we planned to visit the zoo to refresh ourselves.'

Rajat brought his scooter to the side of the road and made a quip 'Thats good. Hope everything is fine.' Rajat glanced at Anjan and asked 'He is?'

'Oh I am sorry he is Anjan, Anjan Saikia. He is two years senior to me. He possesses multifarious qualities, a very talented guy.' She gave a chuckle of delight.

Anjan extended his hands and gave a superficial impression of warmth. 'OK' glad to meet you.' Rajat smiled a smile of dry amusement. He shook hand with Anjan and said 'I am her maternal uncle. I am pleased to meet you. Though unexpectedly. 'Why don't both of you come one day to our house for a change in your convenient time. We will have a some nice time and discuss many things over a cup of tea or if time permits you can come for lunch on a holiday.'

Anjan had the ability to make friendship with people easily. Once again his quick writs enable them to bail out of an awkward situations. 'Definitely we will love to go'. Anjan had a self satisfied smirk on his face. 'I have heard lot of you from Nandita. I am told Mami has a brilliant culinary skill. We look forward to the opportunity to have an agronomical treat at your place.'

They giggled together. Rajat then kicked start his scooter and dispersed. Rajat vividly remembered that Nandita had told about her affair with another boy about a year back. So far he remembered his title was Das. Now this boy was Saikia, Anjan Saikia. He was obviously disturbed by the quick change of titles. He thought in his mind 'May be Das is out and Saikia is in. May be one was false and the other one is true or both were false because both can not be true at a time.' He ignored the matter as extraneous for the time being. Rajat's first impression of Anjan was gratifying. His initial presumption was that the boy was free and frank and knew the art of conversation.

There was a back to back vacation for two days and Nandita went to Rajat's house to spend those days for a change from the routine hostel diet. That was republic day holiday the next day was Sunday. So she came to Rajat's house for a sleep over. They used to talk to late night when she was there. Rajat, his wife and Nandita were sitting in the living room. Moon light washed the front Varanda of Rajat's house. It was a night of dry winter. The air was harshly cold. Rajat had a fascination for raising a fire place at early night. He had a medium sized iron pan where he put some wood charcoals and a few small dry wooden pieces and lit them. Fire slowly kindled in the crude fire place. Rajat brought that inside the room and put over a tripod. The room became warmer and cozy.

All of them snuggled down under the blanks and sat on the sofa and chair. After some time Rajat suddenly raised the topic of Anjan. 'Nandita' Rajat glanced a smile of joy 'I am very impressed with Anjan. I liked his free and easy manner. He seems to be very smart.'

Nandita flickered a smile and did not say anything. She just gave him a pleasant glance.

'I wish you stick with him.' Rajat again said in an embarrassing tone 'Don't mind me saying that. Actually I remembered, you once said that you had an affair with another boy about a year back. I am puzzled. Next to your parents and brothers I am your devoted well wisher. My concern is your future. I am saying this for your own good.'

It had been a discomfiting situation for her but she managed to hide her nervousness and raise a smile. 'Uncle' Nandita chuckled 'You seems to be very serious'

Rajat met her gaze and she dropped her head and wanted to say some things but Rajat intercepted her instantly.

'No, No' Rajat shook his head and he said looking straight to her 'I am your uncle alright but at the same time I am your local guardian. I have a responsibility to know your conduct. Please don't miss understand me.'

Nandita was amused to see how seriously the topic is heading. She raised her hands and said in sobre tone. 'Yes Dipankar Das is our classmate and he is topper in our class all along. Very brilliant. A studious and serious student. But he is very dull and old fashioned person. We were never in deep intimacy, which may be termed as a love affairs. I just had some entertaining time passed with him. He helped me in my studies. But you know he appeared to be quite funny at times.' A flicker of a smile crossed her face.

Rajat sighed with relief that some worry got shirked off from his head.

Nandita said confidently. 'Anjan is a gifted genious. An all rounder you can say. He is formidably intelligent, well read and cultured boy. He knows how to enjoy life with full of promise.'

'I am delighted to learn that' Rajat said with a happy smile 'But please maintain seriousness in such relations. Girls are very vulnerable in this male dominated society. People blame them in a slightest pretext. There is an element of risk. Be careful.'

Nandita shook her head in agreement.

There was a deafening silence in the room. Rajat's wife then blatantly asked Nandita 'So you are determined to make him your life partner.'

Nandita giggled nervously and blurted 'Mami, you are really flamboyant. Easy mami, have patients.'

Rajat waggled in his chair. His wife could derive what he was thinking. She went inside and entered the kitchen. Whenever Nandita came to stay with them, Rajat's wife prepared some very delicious food. She had a natural aptitude for cooking. Nandita got up and followed her inside.

Rajat's wife heard footsteps behind her. She turned. 'Oh! Nandita!' She looked at her quizzically. 'Why did you come? You could have stayed there.'

'Mami!' Nandita threw her arms around her neck 'I have come to see what is the dish for the night.'

'Oh! today you will have nothing special. Because we were not really expecting such an exciting news else we would have arranged a party.' She smiled exultantly.

'But Mani' Nandita giggled 'I should learn how to cook, because ultimately, a girl has to be in the kitchen. Hence I have come to watch you preparing food.'

Rajat's wife let out a loud guffaw. She pinched Nandita's cheek playfully. 'Our doctor need not learn cooking like an average women. You will have people to cook for you.'

'No Mami' Nandita gave a satisfying smile 'All activities are important. We must realise dignity of work. There is also pleasure in acquiring the skill of making tasty dishes. By the way what special you are making to night.'

'Come' Rajat's wife hold her hand 'I have made mutton curry.'

Suddenly Rajat's wife said 'which is the most favourite dish of Anjan? One day, you bring him for lunch.' Nandita was delighted in the thought of the brilliant days ahead. She was plunged into her reverie for her illusory world.

(8)

O, wind, if winter comes, can spring be far behind

- *Shelly*

If winter comes can spring be far behind. Cuckoos gave the news of arrival of spring. Tender green bursted from the trees which were drenched by stormy shower to welcome Rongali Bihu the biggest festival of Assam. For a couple of days the sounds of drum, the rhythmic Bihu songs would keep the state reverberated. State would be fully mugged in festive mood.

Banibrata came from Maniktola a two days ahead of the arrival of Nandita. Rajat planned to come with family including four year old son Raju. He was really very naughty. Kakati's house sprung into excitement and they were happy to welcome this naughty young guest to their lonely quiet hermit. Rajat had a domestic maid Minu. It was a challange for her to keep boisterous Raju amused. She was the one who was most excited to come to Barsila. She found the city life very monotonous. All the day she had to remain inside the home like a prisoner. No one to talk or to play. She fantasized the place in her mind, that there will be a thin rivulet flowring through the green field, mango trees and green foliage in the surroundings. Glistering green smeared over everywhere. There will be large water bodies where ducks will be splashing merrily. She would take bath by dipping in the pond. She wanted that some young boy could get a glimpse of her newly attained youth. She dreamt that young boys would peed from behind the tree to watch her grown up womanhood and they would give her seductive gaze. She imagined that she would be able to enjoy her stay in the village.

Rajat's family members walked down to Kakati's house after getting down from the bus. Rajat was quite young at the time of the marriage of his elder sister. Since then he used to visit Barsila frequently. So he was fascinated with Barsila, with the expanse green paddy fields and blue hill at the northern horizon. Memories of the past echoed in his mind. He had a few friends with whom he used to play during those days. They use to go for augling. When they reached the wooden bridge ahead of kakati's house he showed the stream below to his son and told how he used to catch fish there. When the net was thrown the small fries jumped all over like birds startled by a gun shot. His heart romanticised at the sight of the grassy meadows on both sides of the earthen road.

Rajat observed that the red flowers of Krishna Chura tree had almost shrouded green compound of Kakati's house. Rajat remembered how Kakati used to write the hymen on the greyish green leaves of Mesua ferrea (Nahar) tree. Which was standing in their compound in a fascinating manner. Its beautiful pink to red flash of drooping young leaves. Kakati wrote the following hymn on the green leaves and placed them on every door of the house.

Deva deva Mahadev
Nilagriba Jatadhara
Baat bristi harangdev
Mahadeva Namastute.

The entire house of Kakati came back to life after their arrival. Raju was on his feet since the moment he reached there. He shuffled around the compound restlessly. Minu had a tough time to control him. At times she was so much irritated that she gave him an ear bashing. Minu was depressed that for Raju she might not be able to enjoy Bihu in full vigour.

At the time when all of them were busy in conversation Nilima Kakati's eyes were soaked with tears. She rubbed her eyes and was trying to hide her emotion silently. Nandita touched her and said soothingly 'Maa you are still thinking of Madhabi. God had not blessed her with long of life, So she has left us. Though sad, we must accept God's will gracefully. We could hardly do anything about that. How long you will remain Life has to move with what ever we have with us.'

It was not true that Nandita forgot her all together. Her last words at the time of deporting echoed in her mind relentlessly all through. But she did not show and kept her grief hiden to herself. She asked her mother to focus on the fact that the presence of all the family members had converted their house into a delighted place. Banibrata had already made all arrangement of special sticky rice, curd etc. Nilima Kakati called a woman of the village to help her to grind rice and make traditional cakes, coconut round balls etc. for the occasion of Rongali Bihu.

On the day of 1st day of the Assamese new year all of them wore new gamochas and dresses, they touched feet of the elders and enjoyed the creamy curds, rice flakes and golden syrup. After the lunch all of them sat in the living room and started conversations covering broad spectrum of interests.

During the course of discussion Gobinda Kakati disclosed the affairs of Banibrata and Malabika. Rajat, his wife and Nandita sprang a surprise. They asked Banibrata to reveal the details to quench their inquisitiveness. Banibrata never felt so embarrassed in his life. He gave a shy smile and told 'Malabika is my collegue in Maniktola College. She is the only child of Prasanta Barua a retired engineer and a resident of that place.' She is M.A. in English?

The news was a sheer bliss to Nandita. She was swayed with excitement and greeted him with a smile 'Dada do you have her photo with you?'

Debabrata went inside and brought a group photo taken for their college magazine. Deciphering of her look was difficult but everybody were reasonably impressed with her apparent beauty.

In his excitement to show Malabika, Banibrata then urged his mother and Nandita to make a visit to Maniktola shortly if possible. Though the proposal was attractive yet Nandita opted out because of her studies and final exam. Banibrata requested his mother to go with him after the bihu.

Rajat and his wife were very much excited to hear the news. They congratulated Banibrata. At the same time they were very much anxious to know whether girls parents had consented to the proposal.

Banibrata shook his head dejectedly 'No, Not yet.' He gave a wory smile. 'My impression is that there are still lots of problems. Her parents are very much boastful for her. They are under the illusion that only some rich boy from abroad is suitable for her. I am worried that they, will never accept me gracefully. Lets see what's stored in future.'

'That's right' Rajat sceptically said 'At this stage do you think it will be proper for your mother to go there? Is it not a bit premature? I think she should go after her parents give consent to the relationship.' Else she might meet with serious embarrassment.

'Yes' Kakati supported Rajat 'I also agree with Rajat's view. It sounds prudent. Both the house should agree to the relation and then discuss details of the marriage proposal.' Gobinda Kakati's decision was final. He advised Banibrata to obtain consent from Mala's parents. He further emphasised 'Marriage is most pious relations. Blessings and good wishes of parents and well wishers are very important.'

At night Rajats wife and Nilima Kakati were in the Kitchen preparing to serve dinner. Rajat's wife asked Nilima Kakati in a lighter mood. 'Baideo, which one you think to hold earlier, Bani or Nandita?'

Nilima was completely taken aback. The matter of Nandita's marriage didn't occur to her mind at all. Thought of her marriage escaped her notice till then. It was all very sudden to her. A feeble mention made her senses reel. 'Yes, We must think for her marriage too. We must ascertain if she has some one in her mind. She also might have some affairs too.' She thought in her mind.

Nilima Kakati sighed and said in a calm and composed tone. 'We must think for her marriage. But she must also be prepared. She has to complete her studies. We want to see her established as a doctor and lead a happy in life. We have to seek her opinion.'

Nandita sneaked into the kitchen and her arms crept around the neck of her mother. 'I have heard what you are talking about'. Her expression grew solemn. A faint sneer of satisfaction crossed her face. 'There is no urgency of thinking of my marriage. I will have to do masters in some specialised field. Now a days master degree has become an unavoidable necessity to get a professional entry into the medical field. Marriage can wait not the study. So please leave it to me. I am sure I can sort it out at appropriate time.'

Nilima Kakati looked at her quizzically.

Rajat's wife gave a conceding look, 'Thats fine. We are very much interested in your future and thats why we raised the issue Girls should get married at the right age. That is also true.'

Nilima Kakati shook her head sadly. She said slowly 'The condition of my health is wearing out day by day.' Her voice faltered as she began to speak 'We hope with all our heart that things work out for you as desired. You have a great future ahead and we have high hopes for you.' She turned to Nandita in despair and said. Her eyes were noisted. She wiped the eyes with her *chadar*.

Nandita was struck by a sudden thought and she looked forlorn. Day was not far when all of them would leave their parental house. Her parents would be alone in their nest dreaming about their children in utter desolation.

Despite her sadness she did not allow her true feelings to come out and instead she summed up the conversation by saying 'Let's see what does the future hold for us.' She then giggled and joking by said.

'One thing I can emphatatically assure you that I will not remain as an ascetic spinster.'

During the course of dinner Gobinda Kakati said in a very thoughtful tone 'Rajat, I am sure Nandita has been doing well in her studies in college. Please keep eye on her.'

'Absolutely, she is doing very fine.' Rajat cleared his throat. 'By the way Nandita has a very good friend Anjan Saikia who is two years senior to her. He is a local boy from a good family. Who lives in the city. He is very brilliant and he helps our Nandita very much.'

Nandita who was helping Rajat's wife in serving dinner ran inside the kitchen in embarrassment.

'Oh, that's good.' Bani promptly said 'Have you meet him?'

'Yes for a very short duration. It was very much accidental.'

'Nandita promised to take him to our home shortly.'

'Ok!' Banibrata said with excitement 'Next time I visit your place, I will definitely meet him.'

Gobinda Kakati smiled contentedly.

Rajat's wife came near Nilima and whispered something in her ear.

Nilima Kakati felt a mild throbbing in her heart. She left everything in the hands of God. She wanted to surrender to God and drift her mind away from these serious matters, where God will have the last call.

(9)

Remembering a wrong is the carrying a burden on the mind..

- *Gautama Budha*

After about two years in Chicago, Pradyut shifted to New Jersey where he was working as a software engineer in a multi national company. In New Jersey he meet Robin Barua who was residing there for more than forty years and was an U.S. citizen. Robin was the younger brother of Prasanta Barua of Maniktola.

It was a hot and sunny week end. The front lawn of the house of Robin Barua was covered with verdant green grass. The rediance of garden flowers manifested his pleasing personality. In summer Robin Barua mowed the lawn every week. Pradyut used to visit Barua's house quite frequently in the Friday evenings. Robin's wife was a very hospitable and a courteous lady. Barua liked Pradyut and he had a mind to find a suitor for his niece Malabika and was looking for some promising smart young guy dwelling in the states but was not successful.

During the course of conversation Robin mentioned about his niece Malabika to Pradyut. He had a strong belief that after knowing about Malabika, Pradhyut would be more than happy to accept the proposal. He responded and told Robin that he will bring the proposal to the notice of his father shortly.

Pradyut's father Parbati Kumar Phukan was a retired civil serviant from the State Government and settled permanently in Guwahati. His daughter was married and lived in Guwahati. His wife died two years back leaving him behind.

After retirement he did not have any social engagement. He was an supercilious person and did not have many friends. He was however a voracious reader and books were his best friends and he spent most of his time with books. His other hobby was to promenade in the morning which was followed everyday ceaselessly, because he had a firm believe that walking will keep him fit.

Parbati Kumar Phukan was a man of obstinate behaviour. He couldn't stand to any disorder or indiscipline be that among friends or society. Nobody could read the news paper before he had done with that. He had a special weakness for the smell of the fresh news paper. 'News papers should be as fresh as the news', he would repeatedly say. He was very fastidious in time, dress, food and conversation. Everything should be meticulously perfect and should suit his taste. He got annoyed with all sorts of vexation.

Once a very close relation sent him an invitation for a wedding reception. The host wrote his name as Mr. Parbati Phukan. He raged against the mistake. He spurned the invitation and refused to attend the reception party. Wrongly written name offended him. He was convinced that that could never be a simple mistake. Parbati is a female name which is the name of wife of lord Shiva. Kumar must follow the word Parbati so that his name could mean Parbati's son, that is Lord Ganesh. If Durgadhar is made Durga, Lakshminath is made Lakshmi, Gourikanta is called Gouri they will all loose their gender identities..

Parbati Kumar always went for his morning walk with his friend Hirendra Nath Sarma, who retired as a professor of a local degree college. Only with Sarma he could be at his real self. Phukan strolled side by side Sarma talking about various things of no great consequences. He felt that terrible wrong things are happening in and around their society. He was obsessed with English language and continuously complained about the mistakes he noticed all around. He said in authoritative tone. 'Sarma, have you noticed that they write all wrong English in signboards, in vehicles. He said pointing his hand to a road side hotel. 'See what they have written fooding and lodging. Where they have found the word 'fooding'? Disgusting. What they write in buses and trucks are simply horrible.' After a little pause he again said 'The grandeur of the language has been ruined.'

Sarma was a well mannered man with endearing habit. The friendship between Phukan and Sarma was formed since their college days. Sarma was maintaining a passive role in their relationship and always preferred to compromise for the shake of friendship. He seldom responded.

In some occasion both Phukan and Sarma sit on chairs in front of some shop and discuss many things. Sarma said coolly 'Is there anything we can do to set right all such errant activities?'

Phukan immediately sprang to life 'Why not? We should point out and ask them to rectify. If we all put our efforts in an unified manner the result will definitely come.'

But in most of the days they continued to walk in silence. One day Parbati Kumar said 'Sarma!' He twisted his lips and said 'How could everything go so disastrously wrong? It is a great misfortune that I was born in this lousy place.'

In another day he would come up with a new topic 'You know, Sarma, the Britishers have left this country rather hastily. They should have stayed here for few more years. We were not ready for independence.'

Sarma nodded his head and quietly said 'but independence has also its own charm.'

Phukan stared at Sarma and said 'True. But remember why lord Mount Batten had to stay back in India for ten more moults after Independence. This was necessary to administer the riot torn country consequent of partition. Administration is not children's play. One needs a leadership quality, a commanding of capability.' He gesticulated to show off how knowledgeable he was. He again said 'I am in a sense lucky that my son is in U.S., Those are the place people should live in.'

Everything told to Sarma just went in one ear and out the other. Because Phukan's lectures were boring and monotonous. Sarma acceded to all his idiosyncrasies for the shake of morning walk.

But it was a totally different story with Phukan's son Pradhyut. He had no respect for all the moral values for which his father was prejudiced. The uncouthed behaviour of Pradyut rapidly soared since he landed in Chicago. In a more free society his salacious life flourished more unabated. Within a short spam of time he became very popular among his friends, male and female alike for his drinking and flirting habits. In addition to his physical charm his capability to communicate in English helped him a lot. He forgot the world and thought himself as if he was in heaven. He disdained all social values which were enshrined in our Indian culture. Everything right from food to sex were abundantly available there and Pradyut was busy in dating with girls to satiate his lecherous hunger.

Pradyut did not come home for more than two years. The prime reason was that he married an American girl without any intimation to his family. Actually they were living together with no legal sanctity. Pradyut had a guilty feeling to disclose that ignominious news to his orthodox parents. Phukan and wife were totally shocked when they came to know lately that their son was staying with some girl like husband and wife in Chicago. They were not abhorrent to the girl being an American, but their objection was due to the immoral act that their son was committing. Socially they had never felt so embarrassed in life. Parbati Kumar had not gone for morning walk for few days though that was his most favourite passion. He could not hide his dismay that he had suffered a terrible ignominy. Both parents were apprehended of snide remarks that people might pass on them.

The period of gloom for Phukan's family did not last very long and ended when Pradyut intimated that their marriage was finally fell apart. Simultaneously he left Chicago and shifted to New Jersey on a better opportunity.

'I knew it' Phukan grinned triumphantly and said 'This sort of marriage don't last. These are the result of lust not love. All the attractions vanishes like a puff of smoke after a few months. When both of them find it monotonous. Conjugal life is based on compromise and tolerance. Marriage based on lustful attraction can't last, Marriage is a solemnly divine relations.'

Both Phukan and his wife being relieved of their agony tried to mend their relationship with Pradyut. After all they are parents. They had to forgive whatever indecently their children behaved. They can't disown their son for some wrong doing during his young age.

Mrs. Phukan was a diabetic for several years and was dependent upon insulin. But the lady was naive and careless in taking her drugs religiously. Owing to her prolong neglect after some months she became seriously ill and was hospitalised. She did not respond well to the treatment and after a few days of intensive care she lost hope of recovery. She whispered faintly in husband's ear. 'I know I am close to death. Please take care of Jone.' There was an yearning look on her eyes. His mournful gaze settled on her face. He touched her body which was cold and there was no sign of life. Parbati Kumar Phukan came out of the hospital dejectedly. Death of wife traumatized Phukan and brought discord into the house hold.

However there was glimmer of consolation that his wife got the good news from Pradyut before her death.

After shifted to New Jersey Pradyut came in contact with Robin Barua. He was a perfect gentleman in true sense. Being a boy from Assam Robin developed some affinity to Pradyut and their closeness grew with time.

Pradyut was delighted beyond measure after getting the unexpected proposal from Robin Barua. He was apparently happy about the proposal and he decided to convey the information to his father. Pradyut wanted to take advice from his father in the matter since by then his morally offensive behaviour was waning rapidly and he became reasonably sober. Pradyut mailed a letter to his father on the subject seeking his decision.

Phukan was sitting in his front balcony in the hazy afternoon when unpleasant thoughts kept running through his mind. A light breeze was blowing. The trees were fast coming into leaf. His front garden was full of flowers. He had a domestic servant named Ghanashyam, who looked after all domestic chores of his house. Ghanashyam was a good cook and a good gardener as well. After the death of his wife he became more and more dependent on Ghanashyam. Phukan asked Ghanashyam for a cup of tea.

The postman appeared at the gate and was hesitating to enter. He rang his bicycle bell frantically. Phukan came out slowly and took the letter from his hand. It was an aerogramme and was sent by his son Pradyut. He sat down, opened it and started reading.

Respected Dad,

It's a long time I did not write to you. I appreciate that you have little ground to be happy with my indecorous behaviour. Please pardon me for my misconduct which might hurt your sentiment immensely. I owe you a prefuse apology for whatever I did in the past.

I have shifted to New Jersey on a better opportunity. Here I have met with a respectable gentlemen Mr. Robin Barua. He has been here since more that forty years. He is an U.S. citizen now. There is an important matter why I am mentioning his name. His elder brother Mr. Prasanta Barua was an engineer retired from service and now settled in Maniktola. Their only child Malabika is a lecturer in the degree college there. He has given an idea that we may consider her for me.

Once bitten twice shy. It was a calamitous incident that Killey entered into my life, by some freak of fate. Obviously the impropriety didn't last long.These are all past now. I am hopeful that you will think over with your prudence and experience.

I don't know the exact address of their house at Maniktola. I am pretty sure that you should be able to find that without much effort. It may so happen that you know someone closely from that area.

I solely leave it to you. If you feel that the proposal is well worth considering you may transmit a positive hint. I will be eagerly awaiting for your early response.

Hope you are keeping well. Please continue your morning walk. My regards. Take care.

Yours affectionately
Jone

Phukan read the letter over and again and kept is folded in his study table. His thoughts wandered back and memories of his wife came to his mind. She would have been very happy to see the sense of contrition in the mind of Jone. She would have been in the top of the world. She always was longing for a suitable bride for him and to see them happy. She would have been jubilant to accept the proposal with alacrity. He heaved a sigh of relief.

Phukan was gazing at the blue sky with a soothing dream. Tinge of tears welled up on his eyes. He did not notice when Ghanashyam had put the tea on the table. Time was already up for that cup of tea.

(10)

Glory is fleeting but obscurity is forever

-   Napoleon Bonaparte

A few days passed since Prasanta Barua sent a reply to his brother Robin. But there was no response from him though a considerable time elapsed. Both husband and wife became out of patience. Barua pulled a chair in the bed room near his wife to discuss the matter. 'Robin is a man of words and does not talk superficially. Response should have come by now. May be the Pradyut's family has raised some objection.'

'May be' Mrs. Barua kept the sarees folding on the table and said 'He could have atleast given a call and inform us. God knows whether he has received the letter. Postal Department is so callous that they sometime do not even bother to trace the letter. I think we should once contact him over phone.'

'Right', Mrs. Barua said without taking her eyes out of her sarees. 'I am stricken with fear. Now a days when a proposal of marriage appears the evil eyes befall there and things turned to smoke in the horizon. This is a God sent proposal. There is no dearth of jealous people around. Enemies are everywhere. Nobody can be trust in these matters. Even walls have ears.'

There are various standard times zones in America. Robin was in New Jersey and their time was almost ten hours behind that of India. That was saturday. Robin was expected to stay home in the morning. So Barua decided to go out in the evening for a P.C.O. His wife called Barua the moment he was about to cross the door way. 'Please return early. Don't sit in for gossip somewhere and divulge the matter.'

Barua murmured with annoyance because calling somebody from behind was considered to be inauspicious. 'She should not have committed such silly mistake.'

Barua didn't delay and returned home. He entered the gate and stood on the lowest stair of the varandah. His footwear was dipped in mud and he stamped his feet in annoyance. He removed the shoe and hastily walked straight to the wash room. He was making wild complaints in a soliloquy. 'They are raising the road to prevent over flow of water from the drain. Earth filling has made the road muddy and slushy. I fail to understand their wisdom in carrying out road works in the months of early summer. They will sleep in the dry seasons and work during rainy season.'

Wife was irritated and yelled at him from her room 'What happen? What's the news? Why are you talking endlessly?'

'Robin has received the letter' he shouted. His words resonated inside the wash room. 'He discussed with Pradyut who in turn will let him know after getting a response from his father.'

'Thank God.' Mrs. Barua looked above and raised her had silently prayed. Relief surged through her. 'May God grace us for this marriage.' She felt a spark of high hopes in her heart.

Coming out from the washroom, Barua reached varandah and reclined in the easy chair and shouted for his wife. 'Hello listen.'

Wife told curiously 'Please wait I am bringing tea for you.'

Mrs. Barua came with tea and biscuit. Both of them sat side by side on the varandah. The mosquitoes are causing uneasiness to them. The house was pluged into darkness. Mrs. Barua however had not switched the light on as she thought a secluded atmosphere is suitable to discuss such private maters. Too much lights make the affair public and affect confidentiality.

'Mosquitoes are great menace.' Barua was scratching his legs 'But have you discussed the proposal with Mala? Everything depends on her now.'

Wife shrug indifferently. 'I hinted casually' wife said 'She told that we should not worry. I didn't go for further into the topic.'

Barua wrinkled his forehead and whispered in a suspicious tone. 'what is she trying to indicate? Why should we be not worried It's high time for her marriage. I feel scary if she has some one else in her mind. Keep an eye on her behaviour.'

'She didn't indicate anything of that sort.' She locked at him with annoyance and said 'I have not noticed any visible weirdness in her behaviour? Neither I have heard any rumour of that nature. She must have said casually. Being a girl why should she say, you arrange my marriage, I am eager to get married.'

Barua's mind was over casted with cloud of suspicion. The thought of her affairs with someone kept running through his mind. Her words 'we should not worry' whirled around in his mind.

After a long await one day in front of his gate Barua heard the bicycle bell of the postman ringing, Barua came running from inside the house towards him very enthusiastically. He thought the most awaited letter which they were craving for almost a month might have come.' Prasanta Barua could not resist his temptation. He opened the envelop while walking to his house and gave a quick glance. His eyes gleamed with excitement. He walked inside with a spring in his legs and stood near his wife. He raised his hand as if he was holding the crown of queen Elizabeth. He opened the letter and started reading word for word. Both of them were euphoric as if fortune sailed on them.

'So' Barua kissed his wife on her cheek and said 'Pradyut has confirmed that he received consent from his father. Father also suggested Pradyut to come and meet Mala once. His father will contact us.'

After a pause he started reading the last part of the letter. His voice had gradually feebled. Robin wrote 'I must not conceal any fact from you, specially in the matter of marriage. Pradyut had married an American girl earlier. But they are separated since more that two year now. There is no legal hurdle as such.'

The information dampened his enthusiasm minimally. He shot her a nervous glance. There was no visible anxiety in his wife's face.

Barua once again read the closing part of the letter in a voice close to whispering.

'There is no legal objection and the matter is of little concern. Unlike our country such things are very common and quite insignificant in those society. Nobody bothers for all those flimsy matters.'

Prasanta Barua did with the letter and he folded the same. He walked to his room and kept the letter in a drawer of his table. Barua looked up with a puzzled frown in his face. 'Fortune smiled on him but with a cost' he felt.

Mrs. Barua walked to the varandah and stood by her husband. To drift away the unnecessary worry out of his mind she said in consoling tone. 'That's a free society. Such things happen. That's a non issue. So, you should not waste your time in such trivialities. Moreover he has been separated from her long before.' She said in a convincing tone 'The most important point is that his father has consented to the proposal. I don't think Mala will also have any objection. She can't be so stupid to refuse such a lucrative offer. This boy is a God's gift to us.' She raised both hand and joined to pray 'God bless us.'

After a few days one afternoon Malabika arrived home earlier than her normal time. She was looking very graceful in her modest attire. Definitely any mother will boast for a daughter like Malabika, a charm of personal beauty. Mrs. Barua just fell asleep but hearing the sound of opening the gate she got up and saw Mala coming inside. She curiously asked 'What's the matter? You have come so early today? Are you alright my dear?'

Malabika put her books over the table and replied. 'No, nothing like that' she was stepping towards wash room to get freshened up. She came back and sat near her mother's bed and said 'There was no class and have you noticed the sky. Its fully shrouded by dark cloud drizzlings begin to pour. I forgot to take my umbrella.'

Mrs. Barua for quite a few days was waiting for an opportune moment to discuss the proposal of marriage with her. She thought that right moment had come. Her husband also left for Guwahati. Malabika appeared to be in a very good mood. Hence the situation was contusive to discuss the delicate matter with her.

Mrs. Barua called Mala to come to her room. After her arrival she patted her daughters hand and said 'look your face and hand are totally suntanned. There is going to be worst weather at Maniktola. Its not a place worth living.'

Malabika gazed her mother in amazement. She sensed that mother was dropping some hint. She didn't say anything and curiously awaited because it was not unusual for her mother to find fault with Maniktola.

After a couple of minutes of silence her mother steered the conversation to the main topic. 'Mala' Mrs. Barua was saying with endearment. 'Your Robin uncle had sent a very good proposal of a boy for your marriage. The boy is staying in America. He is an Engineer working in a multi national company with handsome salary. He is there for more than four years now. Your uncle knows him very closely. His name is Pradyut Kumar Phukan and they are from Guwahati.'

Malabika had a little intuition that such a topic was likely to come up for discussion. She appreciated that as a mother she was rightly concerned of her daughter's marriage. She shrugged in differently and smiled chuckly and looked through the window. 'What did you say?'

Her mother was encouraged and said with a blissful smile. 'I hope you are comfortable with the proposal. We, have to inform our consent early.' There was an amused look on her face. Mother was euphoric. She was confident that her beloved daughter had accepted the proposal.

She continued in a voice as smooth as silk. 'Pradyut's father is Parbati Kumar Phukan. They were originally from Sivasagar. He was a senior bureaucrat in the Government and after retirement he permanently settled in Guwahati. Pradyut has one elder sister who is married and they also live in Guwahati somewhere nearby her father's house.'

Suddenly a mischievous gleam appeared in her face and she said 'Above all his mother passed away about two years back. So free from mothe in law.' She giggled.

Malabika was eagerly listening. Her mother again very casually mentioned 'They are from Ahom Community. Nobody care for these things now a days. Educated and cultured people infact feel ashamed to discuss about castism.'

Malabika was silent and was smiling mysteriously. Some vague memories whirled around her mind slowly. Her thoughts began to crystallize into a definite shape. She asked her mother brusquely to repeat the name again. 'What was the name you said?'

'Pradyut Phukan' Her mother repeated instantly.

Malabika's eyes were suddenly snapped open. Amusement glimmered in her eyes. She said 'Yes, go on then?

'As per Robin' Her mother was little bit suspicious but remained unruffled and said calmly 'He studied in Cotton College and than went to Benaras to study engineering. He is handsome, smart and stylish. He has a and handsomely paid job and also he is the lone hirer of father's property.'

Layer by layer scenes were unfolding and had taken an invincible form. A slight feeling of suspicion crept over her. She asked quizzically, 'What more you know? Tell me his entire biography.'

Mrs. Barua was disappointed and looked at her daughter highly sceptically. 'You mean! You know something? Do you know him?' She asked.

'Perhaps, If my memory doesn't fail me' She waggled in her chair and gave a contemptions curl of lips and answered scornfully 'Unless I am not very much mistaken, I could figure him out.' She nodded and smiled fanity. 'I vividly remember that there was a girl Chandrima Gogoi who was my classmate. She was the gentlest girl among our friends.'

'Is she related to Pradyut?' Mother cut her like a bullet and asked.

'We had a strong belief that a relation would consummate.' Malabika sighed deeply at the thought and said 'Pradyut Phukan was a spoilt brat of a senior officer and was from an effluent family. He first met Chandra in some college cultural functions. Initially we had no inkling that they were in close relations. Gradually their relations turned to a serious love affairs. We were also became very friendly with him through Chandrima. We used to meet him regularly and he used to treat us with tea etc.'

Her mother looked at her with glaring eyes in mystification and said 'why they didn't marry?'

'Because of your virtuous, bright American boy Pradyut had some other plane.' Her voice was low but steady. 'One fine morning he fled away stealthy America to without slightest indication to Chandrima. He kept his plan under the wraps and worked on his errant plan very secretly. He carried with him the engineering degree and a huge wealth gifted by his father. He conveniently forshook Chandrima like sugar cane bagasse.'

'How come she was not aware?' Mrs. Barua exclaimed with disbeliefs, because she doubted the truth of the story.

Malabika sternly said 'Yes, she did not have an iota of doubt that Pradyut will ever cheat her like that.' She adjusted herself in her chair and said 'After reaching America he snapped all contact with all his friends here. With the passing of time Chandrima almost given up her hope for Pradyut. She blamed her fate and became a withdrawn person. She could not believe that she will be thrown out like empty bottle of perfume. Though we all hoped that their affair would eventually end up in marriage but that was an illusion and a deceit. It was a height of dishonesty. All the false promises made by that cheat were only to lure her.'

Mrs. Barua said grimly 'She could have got married somewhere else?'

Malabika gave a short derisive laugh 'Marriage? She is now a schizophrenic patient. She is unable to link thoughts, emotion and behaviour, leading to withdrawal from reality and personal relationships.' She released a deep sigh. 'Parents were making all effort and went from pillar to post for her treatment. medical, ayurvedic, homeo, magical incantation and all sorts of worship and offerings to God. But as destined all went in vain.'

There was stunned silence in the room. After quite some time Malabika broke the silence. 'Almost a year back I went to visit Chandrima with two of my friends. The image of that gentlest and graceful Chandrima was a thing of the past. Her face was wrinkled like walnut. She made a pathetic attempt to smile. It was a nauseating sight. She was living emotionless life of a destitute in confinement. We couldn't stand the pitiful sight for long.'

Mrs. Barua was jolted out of her dream. She was speechless with rage after knowing that the proposal was emphatically defeated and that was an wasted opportunity.

'I think you don't know the rest of his lecherous records.' She waggled sideways and looked out of the window. She said 'He is a flirt. He is used to having girls swooning over him. Finally one American girl hooked him and she forced him to live together.'

Mrs. Barua silenced her with a glare and said promptly. 'But they have been separated long before.'

Malabika looked taut and pale. She felt insulted and a sense of abhorrence crept up in her mind that proposal from a person like Pradyut had come to her.' She said roughly 'She divorced him for his unsavoury behaviour.'

Her mother gave a placating smile and hold her hand. 'Why should you be so filled with hate. In those society nobody bother much for such thing. After marriage all these youthful turpitudes will disappear.'

'Hate means?' Mala felt steel in herself and sneered 'I have not opened up more due to the compulsion of decency. It is high time you give up the concept that everything is best in America. Grass is greener on the other side. It is not prudent to run after material comfort and forget the soul.'

Mrs. Barua was trying to persuade her hoping against hope. She said in soft voice. 'Its upto the wife to keep the house in order. Your affection and care will mend his behaviour.'

Malabika suddenly looked fierce and her face turned crimson. 'You are my mother. How can a mother be so cruel to her daughter. Listen carefully, I'm not going to put myself in the mercy of that treacherous scoundrel. He is a devil in human form.' She sprung to her feet and said 'There is no need to flap in the matter.' She stormed out of the room and was simmering with resentment. She felt indignant the way a proposal had come without screening the entire background of a person. 'Irrespective of their own character boys want virtuous girls as their life partner.' She thought with contempt.

Mrs. Barua was bitterly disappointed. All her reverie began to ebb way and slowly vanished. She laid back dishevelled on her bed.

In end of the game Mrs. Barua found a scope goat in Robin. He should not have made the proposal superficially without knowing the details. There is no reason to misguide and create dreams in our mind. It was not wise to accept everything at face value.' Robin might not be aware of all the disgraceful misdeeds committed by Pradyut. Might be he was unaware of those private scandels which were publicly ignored in those hifi society. He perhaps believed If a girl of like Malabika comes to his life, he would be transformed.' That was however most ardent wish. Leopard can not change its spots.

'All the glitters are not gold.' The comments of Prasanta Barua resonated in her ears. She closed her eyes wearily and resigned herself to her fate.

(11)

Everyone thinks of changing the world, but no one thinks of changing himself

\-   *Leo Tolstoy*

A few crows were croaking unpleasantly since the day break in the front courtyard of Prasanta Barua's house. The pair of doves were perching on the fence and were giving startled squawk. A chick fell down and the crows were trying to prey. The pair of doves were chasing the greedy crows off. Barua came out to the varandah and sat in the chair. He was watching the game going on between the birds. Barua was looking at them without watching and slowly fell into a deep slumber. The normal sleep of night eluded him since a few days past.

Barua sprung up at the sound of the lifting of latch of the Iron Gate. Bolin burst inside in tearing hurry. Bolin was a cunning and a deceitful man with wicket tongue. His figure can be geometrically defined as length without breadth. Bolin entered the house stepping like a camel. He pulled the empty chair near Barua. He was munching his pan tamul and sat back and exhaled deeply and said 'What's the matter? You are not seen in the town now a days. Any sickness dear friend.?'

Barua was calm and composed and did not care to respond.

Bolin curiously asked 'Why? Anything wrong with you?"

'No nothing like that' Barua replied with frozen expression. 'I have not been to the market for few days. Market means expenses. Every day prices of commodities are on the rise.'

Barua although said the words very casually yet he felt mild indifference in his heart because he was sure that Bolin would never swallow his false words. Bolin had a notoriority of loitering and poking around whole day with sensational news. He was an unscrupulous person by nature and was known as repository of Maniktola. Barua was scared about the purpose of Bolin's visit in the early morning.

'Friend' Saikia pulled the chair closer and said with a hero's challenge' I have not come to you in such hurry for nothing. There is a fabulous gift for you. I was restless of pass on the information to you the moment it reached my ear. Fortune smiled at you dear friend.' Spark of shrewdness was hiding in his face.

Barua seemed cold and collected and asked 'What's that?'

'One nephew of my wife stays in England. He is a doctor. Her younger sister's husband's elder brother's son. Very close relation. From some source they came to know about your daughter Mala. It is natural that there will be smoke when there is fire. They told my wife that they are interested.' Saikia said in a breathtaking speed.

Barua shook his head and his thoughts wondered off an another tack. Saikia was nonplussed that Barua gave him a wan look with cold eyes. Saikia could not believe why his friend was not excited after getting such an encouraging proposal. Barua could have wept thinking about what he had missed. He had lost his strength to refuse at the same time he had no scope to accept either. He gave Saikia a sullen glance. He felt like crying with looked dejectedly.

Saikia looked perplexed. He had sensed that Barua was sulky about some major catastrophe. He kept silent for some time.

Prasanta Barua broke the silence. Tears gathered in his eyes. 'Bolin' he said indistinctly. 'I lack foresightedness. I cursed myself for my stupidity. I am repenting now. I should not have settled here in Maniktola. I didn't listen to my wife and friends. They had foresight. I never bothered to care for their judicious suggestions.'

Saikia stopped him 'Prasanta there is no worry.' He touched Barua and said they are not concerned about all these silly things like where you stay, what you did etc. They are broad minded and they are interested in Mala only.

Prasanta exhaled a deep sigh of depression 'There lies our misfortune. She has an affair with one of her colleagues here at Maniktola.'

Frown creased in Saikia's forehead as if he was stung by a worm. He gesticulated a pinch to pluck a bud from plant and he said 'Nip in the bud.' He repeated 'Nip in the bud. Don't delay. Be stern and keep watch. These crooks have their greedy eyes on your wealth and property. They act innocent but their real sinister motive is to set a trap on a rich girl.'

At that moment Barua's wife entered with some tea for them. Saikia smartly changed his mood and gave a fake smile to her. She smiled serenely. Mrs. Barua quietly went inside without joining their conversation.

Both were then started sipping their tea. Barua felt annoyed due to the bibulous way of sucking tea by Saikia. Actually he was feeling discomfort in the presence of Saikia. He crave for remaining aloof for some time with himself. Barua vaguely looked outside and said in a feeble voice 'Everything is destiny. We don't know what is stored in our devine providence. I am almost shattered. I know Mala has been trapped by that Banibrata, son of Gobinda Kakati a retired school teacher from a small village town Barsila.

'Shoo' Saikia blew out air from his mouth with a sound like air coming out from a punctured tire. He was intently watching Barua with piercing eyes. He said with haughty disdain 'See my guess is absolutely correct.' Saikia looked up with a triumphant smile on his face. He squeezed his forehead and pondered for a minute and said 'I think I have seen the boy. Though not ugly yet has a poor riff ruff look. Obviously suffered from poverty and malnutrition at the growing stage. I hate to say but I don't think that he is a match for our Mala.'

Barua was nodding his head in dejection.

'Love' Mischievious grin appeared on Bolin's face. He said in a taunting tone 'These are all foolish talk. The moment they enter in to the family chores all glamour of love will vanish. After few days Mala will feel ashamed of walking with him. Marry in haste and repent later. You don't need much time to come to the reality of life. Please understand that to weld a relationship we need metals of same kind. This age is progressive not retrogressive. Take the matter very seriously. Give a deep thought on the matter. Don't delay. There will be many more girls who will jump and grab the proposal, I mentioned.'

Saikia stepped out of home with the same haste as he entered in. Barua felt a great relief. He was puzzled. Bolin didn't have that much knowledge which he pretended to have. He didn't step into a college. But he became a civil contractor and accumulated some wealth. He was Barua's school days friend. One hand Prasanta Barua became engineer and on the other hand Bolin Saikia became a contractor. Obviously a close friendship grew between them.

Barua came tottering inside the house and confided with his wife. Hoping against hope he asked his wife to prevail upon Mala. But his wife knew her much better than her husband.

She had gritty determination. She knew without a shadow of doubt that all these prophetic warnings will avail no success. On the other hand she was fully aware of the arrogance of his husband. To make him understand would be a futile exercise. She reached a cross road. She went inside to sulk in her room.

Prasanta Barua went out of the room and sat in the varandah again. He was in a vile mood and deeply thinking about what should be his next move to wreck to affairs of his daughter. Inciting words of Bolin Saikia ignited some sparks from the ash gathered and he lit the fire of revenge in his heart. Barua was filled with anger and hatred towards Banibrata and his entire family. He vowed to avenge them and teach them a lesson so that they could never dare to reach Mala again. He stood up and paced up and down in the varandah and anxiously thinking of the stratagem.

He went inside to concretize his plan to threaten them with legal action. He choose Gobinda Kakati as the soft target. 'He is a rustic man and it will be easy to terrify him.

He decided to quench his animosity by writing. a letter to Kakati accusing him for inducing the pernicious conspiracy trick his innocent daughter. He had also threatened not to proceed further and if situation demands he would drag them to court for harassing his daughter. He wrote the letter with ferocity which quenched his urge for revenge and he had a solid sleep there after.

Next morning after his breakfast he whizzed out to the post office in incredible speed to shot the letter without delay.

He walked back home from the post office in a vain triumphant mood and shouted for his wife with a broad grin in his face.

Barua wanted to script their future to meet his imagination. Destiny was amused watching Prasanta Barua who was a mere marionette in His hand.

(12)
Anger is an acid that can do more harm to the vessel in which it is stored than to anything on which it is poured

- *Mark Twain*

It was a dreary winter dry day started with dull drizzly morning. Both Kakati and Mrs. Kakati were inside the house. Both of them were not keeping well. Nandita was also in the house. The birds outside were chirping in their nest over the trees broke the silence of the house.

Suddenly a sound of strangled scream jolted the entire atmosphere around. A young woman came running to Kakati's house wailing in a sprill voice 'Help!'. Nandita opened the door and came out. The wretched guest dropped to Nandita's feet. She was piteously crying. She touched lightly on her head, She was shaking with fright.

'Why are you crying?

'Madam. I am terribly frightened.' She sniffed noisily and turned her head back and said in an awful voice 'They will not let me live. They will kill me.'

'Alright.' Nandita gave a percing look to her woebegone face. 'Come down now. Nobody will come here to attack you. Tell me what's it all about.' She told in an assuaging voice.

'Madam, I am from Gerua village.' She whined 'It's two villages away from here. There was a boy from Barsila, who had some relative in our village. He frequently came there and we met there. After introduction he enticed me for love and about a year back he eloped me and we were staying here like married couple. Initially it was all fine. But slowly his drinking habit soared and his employer started coming to our house very frequently. I was forced to tolerate that outrageous man. But last night he came with his co-workers. They were about four in numbers. All were drinking in our house. I am scared. Suddenly I saw one of them entered my room and jumped over me and tried to rape me. I flee from there somehow. She then made a piteous appeal 'Madam I beg you, give me a shelter. I do not need anything. I will do all the servant's works.'

Nandita was infact searching for a domestic help for her parents. Since Madhabi left the house no one was there to take care of her parents. They were old and weak. She used to visit them more frequently. She had already completed her M.B.B.S. degree and now working as internship. Nandita was sympathetatic to her and decided to keep her in their house for all domestic chores and also to attend her ailing aged parents. 'Ok, we can give you shelter' Nandita told seriously 'You have to take care of my parents with utmost loyality. Don't cheat or create any nuisance here.'

'Madam' She touched her feet 'I am immensely grateful. I will do everything. There will be no scope for complain. I need security and one time meal. That's all.'

All of a sudden Debabrata also came home to spend his vacation after examination break. The gloomy and reclusive atmosphere of Kakati's house turned blissful. The hosue came back to life for a short spell.

Debabrata was sitting in the outside veranda enjoying the fan. About a year back Barsila village was electrified. Immediately after electrification Banibrata came home and executed the internal wirings of the house and fitted fans, lights etc. in the house. Debabrata was discussing with father his future plan. Nandita also intermittently came and joined them. Gobinda Kakati had not seen any place other than Guwahati. He had no idea of Mumbai. How big and large institution like IIT was beyond his imagination. But he seemed to be very delighted when he listened about those places.

'I am planning to take up a job after my graduation. In IIT's campus interview takes place and big reputed multinational companies recruit us. So, I will join and then I will try for higher education abroad.'

'Oh! That's very exciting. Please stick to your goal.' Excitement was shining in Kakatis's face.

Kakati was sitting outside on a chair on the varandah. A post man entered and handed over a letter to him. Apart from the infrequent letters from his sons, nobody sent any letters to Gobinda Kakati. He looked the letter meticulously and to his utter surprise he found that the handwritings over the envelope were unfamiliar.

Kakati's curiosity was aroused by the mysterious letter and he opened the envelop. He was surprised that the letter came from Prasanta Barua of Maniktola. He recollected the name because Banibrata earlier mentioned his name. He was jubilant expecting some good news and started reading the letter with ardent interest.

All of a sudden Kakati started moaning with pain and he began to droop and then slowly he slipped down from the chair. Debabrata and Nandita heard the sound and came running near him.

'Deuta! Deuta!' both screamed and called at the top of their voice. His breathing was faint and slow. Nandita and Deba hold him to the room and laid him down in bed. He walked limping. He closed his eyes wearily. Nandita, Deba and Nilima were stupefied to see what happened to Kakati. Nandita asked Debabrata to go to Barsila to call the doctor to come immediately.

After preliminary checkup it was learnt that Kakati had a mild stroke possibly due to some nasty shock. He had suffered a partial paralysis. Doctor had a detailed discussion with Nandita. The letter was shown to the doctor and they all equivocally were convinced that the letter was the cause of heart attack, because for a docile person like Kakati such type of disgusting blames.

Banibrata reached home next day rushed back home the moment he received the shattering news and all them were unhappy, the way Prasanta Barua had treated them. Eventually Banibrata suffered a sense of guilt and he was trying to make a plan to teach a lesson to Barua for his irresponsible cruel act. All efforts by his mother and sister to placate Banibrata proved futile. Mother tried to console him that whatever had happened was their own misfortune. There was no point blowing up it more. But Banibrata was in no mood to concede to such advice of forgiveness. He was firm in his decision to inflict damage to Prasanta Barua with equal proportion. He took the letter with him as the effective weapon. After the treatment Gobinda Kakati's condition became stable. Banibrata was in haste to go back to Maniktola.

Banibrata was determined to take on Prasanta Barua and in his move for revenge he wanted Malabika on his side. Banibrata left for Maniktola, after the condition of Kakati became stable.

He reached the college quite early and sat silently in the common room and awaited for Malabika. Malabika entered hurriedly and took the register and wanted to leave. Suddenly she shaw Banibrata and came near him. He requested Malabika to come to the college library after her class where they could sit in privacy and confide the incident.

'Mala' Banibrata took out the letter from his pocket and handed it over to her and said plaintively. First you read it and judge yourself.'

Malabika hurriedly went through the letter. Her face turned red in anger and revolt.

'Mala, is this the way to insult some innocent without any basis. The letter had caused dreadful anguish and sorrow. He was a very soft hearted simple person. He is always far from all dishonesty in life.

He could never believe somebody pass on slanderous opinion on him and as a result of that shock he had a heart stroke and now lying in partial paralytic state.'

Banibrata had a glance at Malabika. Her eyes were noist. She couldn't speak anything. She was mortified to realise the nasty act of the father. She beg leave hurriedly hiked home.

She stormed into the house and entered her father's room. She tookout the letter from her bag and pushed that into his hand. 'What is this?' She asked in quavering voice.

Barua's heart jolted when he saw his daughter in wrathful mood and he visualized an encounter with his daughter.

Mala rudely said 'You know very well, what's this. It's the document of your meanness.'

She said insolently 'How could you write such insulting words without caring for the fact. You concocted a story and without any rhyme or reason blamed some innocent person insuch an offensive way.'

'Yes' Barua looked around his face twitching with same and rage. He retaliated in emphatic tone 'My intension was to warn that trickster crook. He should fortwith cut off all relations with you and never dare to dream of you.'

'Why?' Malabika spluttered with indignation 'Instead of abusing that innocent man you should have controlled your daughter first. What prevented you to discuss the matter with me first.'

Prasanta Barua was terribly enraged in paroxysm. 'Thats my concern. I did what I considered right and it's my duty to prevent others from inflicting any harm to my family. I must protect the honour and dignity of my family. I can't remain a mute spectator to someone's malicious design to ruin us.'

Malabika shook her head and said 'Shame on you. Could you imagine how much damage you have inflicted to that innocent man. He had miraculous survival from a stroke and now suffering from partial paralysis.'

'Thats not my concern.' He struged off and said 'The people who attempts to burn others house will get punished by God. Therefore one should think twice before involving into such type of nefarious activities.'

Malabika burst into tears and stormed off from the room. She tucked her head down in the pillow and started crying.

Suddenly her father drove into her room at a furious pace and spat at the top of his voice. 'I am least concerned to these affairs. My last warning to you is that you get away from that ruscal. Hope you understand.' After a pause he again said 'if necessary I will take you out from the college. Donot compel me to take more fierce step.'

'What fierce step you mean?' Malabika stood face to face and stared inimically and said 'You almost killed his father now you will target Banibrata. I will strongly protest such violent act. No amount of coercion can separate me from him.'

A nasty sound rent the air inside. Prasanta Barua did not grasp what he had done on the spur of the moment. Slapping of an adult girl was an unpardonable offence. Malabika stood for a moment panting. Barua felt highly indignant and thirsted out of the room.

Prasanta Barua felt a guilty conscience and stood outside the house motionless stared outside vacantly to the sky alone.

(13)

Keep love in your heart, A life without it is like a sunless garden, when the flowers are dead

- *Osear Wilde*

There seems to be direct correlation between sickness and summer season. As the winter had passed over the inflow of patients into the hospital increased. Anjan was working as a junior doctor and their work pressure increased manifold. In fact the major work loads were passed over to them by the senior doctors.

Anjan and Nandita went to the college canteen to take a break of the duty and sat for some tea. It was their regular activity for last couple of months. There were hardly new subjects to discuss but still they felt refreshed after meeting each other. They were busy talking over a hot somosa and a cup of tea. That was the snacks usually all employees and students relish during their morning break.

'Nandita' Anjan bent his head forward across the table and whispered 'Are you free this Saturday?'

'Why?' Nandita replied in a soft voice.

'I mean' Anjan raised the head a little and said 'If you have no plan to go to Barsila I have a plan in my mind. I have no duty that day. We can go to Shillong.'

'Shillong!' Nandita almost exclaimed.

Actually she had never been to Shillong though she heard a lot about the beauty of the place but she had no chance to go there till then.

'My God!' Anjan quieten her down showing both hands 'Don't shout. Care for the people around.'

'Ok!' Nandita was ecstatic about the idea. She said 'I can't miss that chance. If necessary I will skip my class. 'It will be scintillating experience for me.'

'Don't get excited so much. I have to ask for the car from my dad. Of course, that is a holiday. So dad will gladly allow.'

Nandita curiously asked 'What you will tell your dad?'

'I want to take Nandita for a day long trip to Shillong. As simple as that. I hate lies. My dad is a very open minded man.'

Anjan again said 'To cover one lie it might so happen that we might have to resort to series of lies and finally the truth will be out.'

Nandita appreciated and with a shy smile she nodded her head. 'I also don't support any falsehood.'

'So' Anjan then stumped the table 'The die is cast. Our departure time will be nine in the morning. Can you make it by that time?' After a little pause Anjan again said 'This will be your first time to Shillong, right? You know the road is serpentine and wavy therefore many travellers suffer from nausea. Some even vomit.'

'Don't make me scary'. Nandita gave a disapproving glance.

'No, No,' Anjan said raising his voice 'I actually tried to prepare you. Better to have a tablet to prevent all probability of troubles because if you fall sick and all the pleasure of the trip may be spoiled.'

'Thats ok. I have no problem' Nandita said almost in a whisper 'you don't come near my hostel. I will come out to any convenient location. Because I do not like my hostel mates to guess and cook gossip. The girls are normally very jealous.'

Throughout the night Nandita was dreaming their trip to Shillong. She also felt abit nervous because she was going alone with

Anjan. She didn't go outside the city with Anjan and for that matter with anybody. She could feel her heart beatings which of course she enjoyed.

Sharp at nine in the morning Anjan reached Ganeshguri at the agreed pickup point. He looked out for Nandita but she was nowhere in sight. Anjan glanced at his watch. After five minutes of waiting he came out of the car and raised his head to look the way Nandita was supposed to come. No, there was no trace of Nandita anywhere around. He lighted a cigarette and started puffing very leisurely. After a few minutes Nandita got down from the rickshaw in front of the petrol pump and looked around like a lost child. Anjan smashed his cigarette by his shoes on the ground and came near Nandita. Anjan said to her 'So, today also you failed to maintain time. Come now and sit inside the car.'

'Sorry Anjan' Nandita looked perplexed.

'Anything wrong with you?' Anjan asked looking at her curiously.

'No, No' She was almost stammering 'I came out from the hostel and suddenly the strip of my slingback ruptured. I went back again to wear another pair which is not very formal. It doesn't fit to your style. Would you mind?'

'That's alright' Anjan turned the siritch and the car whizzed along. He said 'I will present one pair at Shillong. Varieties of stylish women foot wears are available in Shillong.'

Anjan was manoeuvring the zigzag turns from one hills to the other. Anjan was explaining her that this road was very narrow and till few years from now vehicles were allowed to ply only in one direction. The traffic control gates were at Jorabat, Nangpoh and Mowlai.

'By the way' Anjan asked Nandita 'Are you comfortable?' I hope you are not feeling nauseous because of the twisty roads.'

'I am fine'. Nandita opened the window glass and cold draft of air entered the car. She inhaled deeply. She was mesmerised and said. 'Anjan all these hills are covered by beetle nut trees creeper plants and other tall trees. There is no habitation or village?'

'In hills the people live in groups in small hamlets. They have their houses inside the hillocks.'

They stopped at Nongpoh and enjoyed the tea and snacks. They strolled for a while looking over the shops. Anjan lit a cigarette while coming out of the tea stall. He was lovingly admonished by Nandita for smoking.

After Nongpho the topography was gradually changing. Tall pine trees were shrouded in mist and dancely overspreaded over the hills. Nandita's eyes were glued to the mesmerising beauty of the lush green hills. She felt chilled wind blowing on her face.

'Nandita enjoy the breathe and calm your soul and treat your eyes in greenery' Shillong is called Scotland of the east.'

Anjan was describing while driving the car. Nandita was enjoying the cool, silent serenity of the surrounding. She didn't say anything. Spoken words are irrelevant at that moment.

After sometime they reached the most beautiful spot of a few kilometre ahead of Shillong, Umium lake, 'Surround by the tall pine and fir trees forest this lake is popularly known as Barapani. It is a sprawling man made lake formed by damming Umium river.' Anjan was explaining her while negotiating with the hair pin bends of the road. They got down on way and soothed their bodies with the charm of the Lake and the ravishingly beautiful surrounding.

Finally they reached Shillong and proceeded to famous Wards lake which is one of the most popular attractions of Shillong. This Lake is also known as Pollock's lake. This artificial waterbody is landscaped with well trimmed lush green grasses and patches of bright flowers in colourful setting.

Nandita was very much excited to move around in the beautiful lake. She was excited to see the coloured fishes. Nandita asked 'What this Ward stands for?' She touched him gently on the arm and they walked along arm in arm.

Anjan explained 'The lake is named after the then chief commissioner of Assam, Sir William Ward, who planned it?'

They went to polo ground where they ware strolling over the green grasses holding each others hand through the tall pine trees. After sometime they sat under a large pine tree 'Let's sit in the shade for sometime to feel the serene beauty of the place.' Thomas Hardy wrote a novel named 'Under the green wood tree.' They sat very close to each other. They touched each other intimately. Their breathing became fast their palpitation rosed. Anjan kissed Nandita profusely on the lips and face. They were motionless for quite sometime and were infatuated by love. After some time they decided to leave for police bazaar for lunch and shopping.

On way back Anjan showed a small round of hillock covered by tall fir trees. Anjan said to himself 'Such a queer romantic place, so poetic.'

Nandita was silently devouring the beauty of the pristine pollution free lush green undulated countryside.

'Nandita' Anjan hold the steering by the left hand and took out his right hand and pointed his index finger towards a hillock and said 'See the beauty of the place. The needle like leaves of the fir trees were gently swaying in the breeze. I love to stay in such serene and saintly place. Just imagine if we build a cottage here and stay. Can you imagine only you and me in a small hermitage, away from the hastle of the city.'

He pulled his hand inside and said again 'Our children will play around in this area?'

Nandita giggled in sarcasm 'Nice reverie, Now stop dreaming and drive safely'. After some pause Nandita again said 'How can we be happy here. There is no life around, No place for entertainments, no society only monotonous loneliness. I don't like such place. I can't imagine that people can be happy in such a forlorn place?'

'I know, I know.' Anjan giggled and said 'There is pleasure in staying away from the bedlams of the city life, a pleasure of roaming in the pathless woods. 'I love not man the less but nature more.' It's from Lord Byron's poem.'

'Many things are good for poetry. Moreover most of these poet's minds roam in illusion and crazy lunatic ideas.' Said Nandita feigning indifference 'That's only fantasy.'

'Ok, Ok, you became serious 'Anjan patted her thigh with his left hand and said with a pleasant smile. 'Now lets drink some tea and snack on the next road side joints. Even lovers have to eat.'

By the time they reached Guwahati. It was late evening. At the end of the day after the sun went down the sky was dipped in by faint red twilight.

After a few days Banibrata made a shocking revealation to Nandita that under no circumstances Mala's parents would see eye to eye with the proposal. 'So we are critically in a cross road. There was no sign of melting.' He informed and said 'Further waiting will be in vain and total waste of time. Things are likely to worsen in coming days. So we have decided to go for registered marriage in Guwahati. Till the completion of the process the matter had to be sworn to secrecy.'

On receipt of that information Nandita became restless. After her class hours went to the duty room of Anjan and called him by raising her hand to come out for a short while. Anjan dashed out from the room.

'What's upto?' Anjan looked at her anxiously.

'Anjan, There is something very urgent matter to discuss with you. Can you find some time right now so that we can talk freely.'

'Alright I will meet you after some time. Let me wind up my duty.'

Both met at college canteen. Nandita failed to hide her nervousness 'Anjan!' Nandita gave a wary look 'The issue of dada's marriage becomes a matter of great concern.'

Anjan interepted her and said 'Look this is a crowded place and not at all conducive to discuss such secret affairs. Let go to Panbazar in the evening and we will talk there in details.'

Nandita and Anjan went inside a restaurant in Panbazar and they selected a table at rare corner. They ordered for chicken cutlet and coffee.

'Anjan' Nandita said very seriously in faint voice sipping over her coffee 'You are aware that Dada has an affair with Malabika, one of his colleagues in the same college. But her parents are bitterly opposed to their relationship. Her father is an obstinate man. In fact he has put severe pressure including physical assault on her to forcibly sever all relations with dada. He has insulted our father and slapped absurd allegation of inciting dada in his alleged malicious motive. They seem to be staunchly adamant and not inclined to listen to rationality.'

'Strange' Anjan twisted his lips and said 'Both of them love each other. They are of same profession. No transfer they will stay in same place. They will have holidays together. What for this objection? What her parents want?'

'Actually love marriage in their circle is unprecedented.' Nandita was looking straight ahead and said 'Moreover Malabika is very good looking and charming as I am told. She is very talented as well and above all she is the only child. So parents are very proud of her and are keeping high hope for her. They boast that relations from abroad will only be considered for her. Nothing less than that.'

Anjan laughed. 'Snobbish people. Completely obsessed with foreign. They imagine America as heaven.'

Nandita again said 'They consider us to be economically inferior to them.'

'Ridiculous' Anjan gave a soothing look and said 'True your father doesn't possess a huge wealth but he has three precious gems. Professor, doctor and youngest one is a graduate from I.I.T. Bombay. What an enviably ideal family. They are actually uncultured foppish.'

Nandita's face was visibly anxious at the thought of court marriage. She said 'It's frightening for me. I have never heard of such thing with any of my known person. I am terribly worried.' After a brief pause she laid her hand over Anjan arm and said again said 'Malabika now seek our support and help. Both of them want to come to Guwahati to register their marriage in the court. She has already contacted husband of one of her friends, who is a lawyer here. But everything has to be done in secrecy.'

'Good' Anjan calmly said 'What help should we are supposed to offer?'

Nandita glanced out side through the window an thoughtfully said 'I think its not very complicated, they need us to be with them. They are also perhaps scared and need some moral support. They should feel that what ever they have decided, their family and well wishers are right behind them.'

'Don't worry' Anjan blissfully assured 'I will be with them during the process. I mean I will provide necessary logistic support to them if necessary. Its difficult to win an argument with such type of obdurate people, because they only listen what suits them. Lets keep our hope upon God. Trust Him.'

Nandita breathed a sigh of relief after hearing the encouraging words from Anjan. 'Thanks' Nandita said effortlessly. Nandita silently prayed God to shower blessings to her brother and Malabika.

(14)

**All human actions have one or more of these seven causes
nature, compulsions, habit, reason, passion, desire**

- *Aristotle*

Debabrata left for joining into his job with the multi national company at Mumbai. It was a long and tedious journey. Only in the morning two passes plied from Barsila to Guwahati. Then from Guwahati to Howrah by train. From Howrah to Mumbai by Gitanjali Express. The end station was Victoria terminus. From there again by local train to Powai. From Powai station to take a rickshaw to reach IIT campus. The entire journey took three full days. He will have to collect his belonging from there and to shift to a rented accommodation. Nandita also left home for medical college to attend to her duties. Only Tara was there to look after her ailing father and frail mother. Loneliness helplessness which made her mother disconsolate were of great worries which were haunting her mind frequently.

It was a hot dry summer. The sun blazed down from a clear blue sky. Nandita had an exhausting day at work. She came to her room in the hostel and sat under the fan to get relief from the scorcing heat pouring from the dazzling sun..

She heard faint sound of footsteps on the far end of hallway outside. The sounds became more obvious and were approaching towards her room and finally it came to a halt in front of the door. Somebody mildly knocked the door. Nandita was puzzled because her roommates never bothered to knock but dashed inside. She stood up at unaccustomed incident and opened the door. She greeted the unexpected strangers and requested them to come in. Nandita let her gaze wander. The taller and the fairer one with an affable smile looked at her and stretched her hand 'If I am not wrong you are Nandita?'

Nandita was amused to see how a stranger could recognize her. For a moment she felt herself like a celebrity and she looked at them quizzically and politely asked. 'Excuse me, I have not been able to place you.'

The other lady slighty dark and fat, opted to introduce and said 'She is Malabika from Maniktola and I am Rehena from Ulubari, Guwahati. We are very intimate friend's since our college days.'

Nandita felt embarrassed at being the centre of attention. She could not imagine that Malabika would appear before her in such a surprise. She pulled two chairs and requested them to sit. Both of them eased themselves in the chairs. Means while she tangled up the sheet on the bed as she quickly lay tossing and turning.

'Please make yourself comfortable while I get some tea.'- Nandita said wit a bemused smile.

'Nandita don't get tense, we all had experience of our hostel life.' In the contrary your room is much better than what we had in our time.'

Malabika rosed from the chair and pulled Nandita to sit on the bed. Don't bother for tea. 'We have just had our lunch. My friend Rehena made delicious food. We are full.'

Both Malabika and Rehena giggled. Rahena added 'Don't believe her. She has a habit of extolling others.'

Nandita asked pleasantly 'Anyway when did you come? Anything to do with treatment and you want to consult some of our professors. Or something else?' Though she had an inkling of her purpose to come to Guwahati yet she throught it prudent not to disclose that and therefore she reaised a totally irrelevant topic.

'Nandita' Malabika touched her hand and chuckled 'Not at all doctor Madam. We are perfectly healthy.' My sickness can not be cured by the doctors it's in the domain of lawyers.

The sole purpose of Malabika to come to Guwahati was to consummate their marriage through registration in court. The moment she heard it her blood ran cold. She was infact scared of this event all along. 'A marriage without the blessings both families and well wishers, keeping aside all customery paraphernalia.' She pondered.

'When you propose to execute the registration?' Nandita asked and she was over taken by the speed of events. But one need to speed up to win the race. 'But' Nandita asked 'There will no elders to bless. Is it not a very casual sort of thing?'

Her pointed question made Malabika discomfit. Her remark was followed by an embarrassed silence. Malabika knew very well that marriage is a sacrosanct relationship and blessings of parents, elders and well wishers have immense value. Everybody expects such auspicious things to happen in their lives and in almost all cases nobody is ever deprived of these. But though very rare yet some unlucky girls miss these things which are mostly because of parents irrational arrogance.

'Yes Nandita' She had a guilty look on her face 'Every girl aspire for that. Nobody likes to ignore the parents. But unfortunately some people are so unlucky that they need to fraught with dreadful things. My family is aggressively adamant. They are obstinate to arrange my marriage with someone of their choice. They are absolutely materististic and in no mood to listen to reason.'

It saddened Nandita that people could be so cruel. People blindly hanker after money and fame all their life. They think only wealth can earns happiness. The human ego is the ugliest part of man.

'Your brother has already discussed with Maa and Deuta. They have accorded their consent and encouraged us to go ahead. They accepted that in the absence of any other options court marriage is inevitable. They also suggested for early completion of the formalities. There is no point in con centrating on the closed door and miss the open one.' Malabika was explaining the situation.

Malabika again said 'Moreover Maa and Deuta have agreed to carry out the religious rituals and to give a wedding reception at a convenient time later.'

'That's fine' Nandita said with jubilation 'Our relatives and friends will be happy to attend the marriage. By the way when dada is coming?'

Malabika replied with a contended smile 'How can you play Hamlet without the prince of Denmark. The prince is arriving tomorrow. He had gone to Barsila to take blessings from Maa and deuta. Everything has been planned in fastidious details but stealthly. It's a mater of one hour or so in the court.' She patted her friend Rehena's back and said 'Her husband is an efficient lawyer. He has already completed all preliminary formalities.' After a little break. Malabika again said 'So I request you and Anjan to be witness to the proceedings.'

'My husband actually repeatedly told me that it will be good to have some people as witness other than family members. So you please persuade Anjan to come.' Rehena said will joyous laughter. 'We will celebrate the wedding after the registration is over.'

'I will definitely be there. Anjan has already agreed to join. Please let me know the timings. You can contact me evening in our hostel telephone.' Nandita again said 'Oh! Before I forget, Anjan told me to tell him if you need any transport etc.'

'Alright' Malabika gave a pleasing look and taid 'So kind of him. Hopefully we will be able to manage. Actually his presence is more than enough. We will feel an aura of solidarity.'

After some general conversation Malabika and Rehena got ready to leave.

After the registration of their marriage. They all went to a restaurant and had celebrated the occasion. Rehena and her husband beg leave of them after they had done with enjoying the treat. Nandita accompanied the newly wedded couple to the temple of 'Maa Kamakhya' to take blessing from Goddess.

The marriage of Banibrata and Malabika was actually a legal recognition, which they performed to protect them from any evil conspiracy of the people in opposition. They decided to stay at Maniktola for few more day separately like before.

After about a month Banibrata arranged a formal marriage at Barsila with all religions and customary rituals. In the evening there was a wedding reception. Kakati's house was jubilant. All invities flocked to Kakati's house to grace the occasion and bless newly wedded the couple. People were charmed by the beauty of bride Malabika. 'She got a very pretty face' 'an exquisitely beautiful bride.' An appealing beauty. 'She is very attractive.' The bride and groom were showered with compliments and blessings. The members of the family gave a graceful bow to the guests as an act of genuine humility.

(15)

Love does not claim possession but gives freedom

-    *Rabindra Nath Tagore*

Bolin Saikia failed to feel his age and his wily feat did not waned. Residents of Maniktola, old and young alike knew him for his wicked tongue because when ever some iniquitous and exciting news, reached his ears, he became restless. He had special interest in gathering snippets of personal affairs of others like whose daughter always came home late, who moved with whom, who had eloped whose girl etc. Special interest was for news with illicit flavour. So for him a news like Malabika's court marriage which was the first of its kind in his domain of his knowledge was a God sent. He was thrilled and ran to his wife with a self satisfied smirk on his face. 'Hi! Just now I got an explosive news that princess of Maniktola fled away and got married in the court at Guwahati. Shame, shame. It's a disgrace to Maniktola. It has duly hit the pride of Mrs. Barua. It's now time for Prasanta to swallow his pride.' I am impatient to meet Prasanta.'

His wife put her index finger on her lips and implored not to go to Barua's house. She pleaded 'Barua is your close friend and Malabika is like your daughter. You should not make fun of such an unfortunate happening. Barua and his wife must be feeling terribly depressed. You should console them at this moment. Try to realise the situation that might be going on in their family. We should not take sadistic pleasure on others misery.'

'Why?' Bolin gave an evil grin 'Have you forgotten how proud her parents were? It is a great slap on the face of that swaggered lady.' He again repeated glinting his eyes. 'This marriage ultimately ruined her parents.' He took a step towards the door and went out by saying to himself 'I am going to Prasanta's house.' He stormed out murmuring. 'Our Mala is stunningly beautiful. Her match must be in America or England. Downfall is imminent to haughty people.' He smiled radiantly.

Bolin entered Prasant Barua's house with a galloping steps like an overacting comedian. Barua was sitting on a chair in the front varandah looking blankly outside. His mind was in a whirl. Seeing the poker faced Bolin entering into his house Barua's heart started pounding. He thought he had for sure come to rub salt in the wound.

'Listen friend' Saikia almost bellowed in the ears of Barua something very serious and confidential news. Have you already heard by any chance?'

Barua was in a gloomy silence. Saikia flashed a false smile. He said almost in a single breathe 'Malabika got married in Guwahati. Are you sure you don't know or you have pretended before me?'

Finding Prasanta in consternation he repeated 'Look, I warned you well ahead of time. You did not act in time moreover upbringing of your daughter was also faulty. You reap what you saw.'

For the first time in life Prasanta became enraged with Bolin because of his derogatory remarks which he found very much distasteful and uncouthed. Prasanta Barua was already in low morale. A deep sense of despair devoured him and his wife. He as a close friend should have consoled him at this hour of misery, and instead he was taking all pleasures out of that. He came to add salt in their wound. Barua's anger shot up and he wanted to slap him in his face.

Despite his terrible anger he didn't utter anything, Barma refused to see Bolin eye to eye out of disgust. Bolin Saikia realized that he should push off and he slowly left the house with a steely smile without saying bye to Barua. Saikia's spirit was dampened. He discredited himself because of his failure to be the first person to release the bombshell and to take full credit for his spying skill.

Barua entered the room and sat wearily near his wife. He touched her shoulder and tried to comfort her. He mumbled 'What can we do? It was written in our fate. People are taking pleasure in our misery.' He was close to tears. He said like a monologue 'We have perhaps failed in our duty in upbringing our child. May be it was in her destiny. We have to leave everything in the hands of God. We have no right to judge his judgement. We are but to accept it.' His voice was throbbing with emotion.

Barua left the room rubbing his eyes with the back of his palms.

Malabika came back home from Guwahati after registration of their marriage. The house was engulfed in remorseful silence. Mother gave her a sullen glance. Her parents were avoiding her either to make her feel that they were furiously enraged or they wanted to hide their disappointment. There were no exchange of words with her for few days.

On afternoon as usual Malabika came back from college and went inside her room. She was sitting on her chair in a gloomy silence. Her mother stormed into her room and started scolding her in top of her voice. 'Disgrace to your education. Is it the value of your moral education? You have thoroughly ruined our prestige. We cann't go out and face people. We have to hang our head in shame. We have never been so humiliated in my life.' She started to sob uncontrollably. 'We had an absolute dream. It is a shattering blow to us. All our hopes and dreams ended for your senseless act.'

Malabika had lot of reasons to react but she hold back. She thought silence is golden. She did not want to add fuel to the fire.

Her mother did not stop. 'Before resorting to such a horrible things could you not think about us, about the society and hesitate for once?'

She was hesitant inside the court. She had almost broken down. Nandita was holding her and stood in support. Nandita said,

'Circumstances compelled you to take this unusual step. You had no alternative. You have a life, your parents should have realised that. You can't always live a life for others.'

Malabika's mind was in whirl. Why the parents want their children to blindly comply to their wish. Grown up children also have right to decide about their future. Children are not their puppets. Mothers remarks stung her into action.

'Maa' She turned to her mother. 'Don't be foolish. You have never bothered for my feelings. my likings, my life. You have treated me as a precious asset, a highly priced marketable item. All these for your selfice interest to satisfy your ego.'

Banibrata and Malabika hired a house in the town and started staying there. They had thrown a wedding reception in their new house among the colleagues and some well-wishers including the shop keeper from whom he used to buy items on credit. On the other hand melancholy descended to Prasanta Barua's home. They became withdrawn from their normal social contacts. Some friends and relatives did visit them but they were sceptical about the inner motive of the people.

But nobody can stop passing of time. Time withered the sulky esteem of both sides. They all got good counselling from their well-wishers. Dictates of reason take a long time. Bondage of marriage is so powerful that all bitterness gradually swayed into insignificance. How long the ego could strive before a relationship like marriage? How long one can stay in a state of self denial? Truth is great and will prevail.

Barua couple also slowly started deeply thinking the issue in a sensible perspective of a happy and contended life. Forgiveness is the best form of love in any relationship. Nobody can escape such eternal special bonds of relations. Malabika meant everything for them. They had deep introspection into the entire thing to come to a more pragmatic decision. Love triumphed over everything else. One has to look realistically at the world around us. It was highly embarrassing to live in same place, like strangers in such a small town. There was obvious possibility of meeting each other every now and then. People would relish to smear gossips on their relations. Wisdom prevailed upon parents of Malabika and they had decided to forgive and accept Mala and Banibrata. Everything happens as per destiny. They finally wanted to give a respectable shape of the entire episode and to burry all misunderstanding. What can not be cured must be endured. Ultimately an atmosphere of acceptance, tolerance and compassion prevailed upon both the houses. All ill feelings that happened in past were obliterated from their memory. Love conquers all Bama consoled himself, 'When all is lost future still remains.'

(16)
Do not he led by others, awaken your own mind, amass your own experience and decide for yourself your own path

-   *Atharva Veda*

Social customs, social concepts transform with the passing of time. New habits, fashions replace the old traditions. In the late afternoon Gobinda Kakati was sitting in the front courtyard feeling obscurely amused over the changes he had witnessed throughout his life. Sun was creasing in the west horizon and slowly the sky turned gloaming. The birds flew back to their nests. He wondered about the instinctive magnetic pull towards their nest. Perhaps safety and security are prime concerns which pull the birds to their nest. There were all kinds of thoughts running through his mind.

Debabrata already got a job in a multinational company through campus interview and his posting would be in Mumbai. Kakati was convinced that he would have a promising career. He will shine in life. Huge number of birds had flocked in the tree and were chirping to clutch their respective places. Everybody in this planet are battling for same competition in life.

The sky was clear and lit in twilight. Gobinda Kakati after a light stroll in the compound came inside house using his stick and eased himself on a chair. Tara was putting the lights on. Mrs. Kakati came near her husband and sat on another chair close to him. The house was silent barring some feeble sounds created by a few birds outside and Tara in the kitchen.

'Deba is stepping into a new life' Kakati was farely able to stammer out the words. 'I pray God to grace him good luck.'

Mrs. Kakati did listen but did not respond. She had almost withdrawn herself from all attachment of life. She was dithering over what to say. She said 'How does it matter? He has left us forever.'

Gobinda Kakati consoled her 'The parents bring up their children, and when they become able to stand on their own, they leave the nest. This is the law of nature.'

Nilima Kakati spent her day either by sleeping, or by dozing. There was a worried expression on her face, and most of the time she preferred to be reticent. She seldom shared her thoughts with Nandita also. She had observed that one by one her children have deserted the house which was once a place full of hope and aspiration. Now the house turned to be a recluse and seldom come to life. That became a forlorn place.

Her only prayer was 'Oh! God, take care of my children wherever they may be.'

Nandita arrived home. Nandita was overwhelmed with feeling of forlornness. She found her home in a sadly gloomy atmosphere. Her anguish filled her heart. She was at a loss what to do with the situation.

Kakati got up and greeted her with embrace. Kakati also tried to throw a smile hindered by his paralytic nervous system. They looked very happy whenever she came home.

Nandita's mind was in a vexation with a loads of thoughts. How these two aged infirm persons would live in such a lonely situation? One day one of them will pass away leaving the other. They might be thinking who will leave earlier. Nilima Kakati expressed once that she wanted to pre decease her husband. She might appear being far too pessimistic. Actually suffering loneliness, sorrow, disappointment and death are part of our journey. Death is the permanent solution of all problems. No body likes to discuss those scary things.

Thoughts of consequences of impending loneliness of her parents had hovered over her mind and she is feeling terribly helpless. Nandita became stressful to think about the situation of despair in her home. More she thought for a solution more her mind slipped to perilously disastrous situation. Her thought met with the dead end.

Gobinda Kakati usually got out of bed early. He strolled a few steps temping in the front Varandah. After that he eased himself and sat down on a chair. Tara used to give him a cup of tea and a couple of biscuits.

The crow outside the house were making unpleasant noises the might see some cat or civet around. Sound reached a frightening proportion. Nandita came out to see what's wrong with the crows. Coming events cast their shadow before. It was shocking Kakati was sitting in the chair motionless. His body was dangling on one side over the handle of the chair. Nandita was at a loss, She was terribly frightened and started screaming.

'Deuta', 'Deuta'. She shouted. Her lips quivered and then she started to cry. Nilima Kakati heard the screaming and rushed out. She was unable to comprehend the situation. She saw her husband drooped motionless. Nandita clung on her mother and both of them started sobbing uncontrollably. She examined his pulse rate and heart beat and was certain that Govinda Kakati wraped up his role in this earth very peacefully. There was no troublesome transformation from life to death. The doctor came and declared him dead.

The moment the news of Kakati's death broke out the people of Barsila, poured in to get the last glimpse of Kakati and to pay their respect. Banibrata and Malabika dashed off home. It was a bolt from the blue for them.

Kakati was a paralytic patient but he could manage with the support of medicine. He followed a strict routine life till his end.

Never in his wildest dream Banibrata imagined such a sudden demise of his father. There was of course a great consolation for Banibrata that the he didn't have to suffer prolonged pain normally associated with death. It was a peaceful death. The quiet and peace loving man had left them peacefully. That was their consolation.

It was a very crucial decision for Debabrata because has just joined his service. He was absolutely divasted by the news. It was a very tricky situation and his friends were also not sure what would be the right thing to do. It was true that even if he takes a risk of loosing the job he will not be able to extend any help. After some arguments he decided not to rush to Barsila. Debabrata tried to console himself and wrote a letter to his mother.

Dear Maa,

I am utterly disturbed and mentally devastated on receiving the saddest news. I don't know how to console you when I myself am unable to control my grief.

I can't imagine that I will miss my most respected Deuta forever. It's an irreparable loss to us. At this hour of bereavement I should have been near you. But as illuck would have it I couldn't even do that. I curse my misfortune. Maa please forgive me. I have full confidence that dada, bou and baideo are all right behind you. I hope to get leave for a short period. I will have some time to stay with you. Hope everything will be perhaps over smoothly by the time this letter reaches you.

No matter where I am, the spirit of my father will be always beside me. My appreciation of my father's greatness can not be measured. His guided will remain for ever with me. Dad, wherever you are, you are gone, you will never be forgotten.

May God rest his soul in eternal peace.

Have faith in God. Trust him. He will find some way to get you out of his period of grief.

My regards. Take Care.

Yours loving

Sarubapu

The customary rituals for the eternal journey of the soul were performed with the help of friends and relatives including the family of Rajat. Large number people, students came to pay their homage to Gobinda Kakati on the day of shradha.

The absence of Gobinda Kakati casted a serious emotional void for wife Nilima. She was by nature an introvert women. After the death of her husband she completely lost interest in life. She resigned herself to her fate. She became apathetic and silent. She imagined that during the rest part of her life she will walk alone in the endless desert.

Banibrata was worried for his mothers. He discussed with Nandita if some companion of her age could be brought in so that she could at least share her emotions apart from a mutual company. Nandita thought that the idea sounded good but there was sincere doubt on its realistic angle. It was not easy to find such a reliable destitute women.

Banibrata had a gloomy expression. He said in a persuading tone. 'I am thinking to take Maa with us for some days. She needs a change more so to stay away from this pathetic sight. What do you think?' He sought advice from Nandita.

'I don't believe she will agree. Idea is not bad. Any way you can talk to her.' Nandita looked highly sceptical. As expected Nilima Kakati respected the proposal. She said 'I should not leave this place for one year from now. This is one of the basic tenets which I have to follow religiously.

They were not confounded since she will not agree to deviate from the prevailing age old social belief.

It was unendurable when Bani and Mala were ready to leave to attend the call of duty. They had painfully noticed the stoical endurance of the loss their mother had suffered. Banibrata was highly down hearted and he could not hold back his tears. Both of them bowed down to touch her feet and turned their head quickly and wiped their eyes. They could not even say good bye. Nandita cried a tearful fare well.

After Banibrata and Malabika left for Maniktola Kakati's house again plunged into a deafening silence. There were days when the house was filled with laughter, arguments, jokes and lots of mischief. All these were now the memory. There was no life there. Everything was calm and peaceful. Nandita was in a terrible dilemma. What to do? She has completed her MBBS degree as usual she should try for a job or to peruse her specialization. It was also essential to join a job to run the house hold expense. Of course till then Banibrata was taking the responsibility of the expenses of house as well as for Debabrata. But expectantly it was her turn to share responsibility to look after her mother. Debabrata had already started earning. So the financial obligation on that front had ceased, resulting a great relief on Banibrata.

The problem of financial hardship was a pie before the problem of physical absence. Loneliness was taking it's toll and it's severity was more for Nilima. Nandita could not gather mental strength to leave her mother alone. Her mother would be would be living a life not lived.

Nandita became deeply thoughtful and she wept thinking why they had been put to such a precarious situation. She earnestly wanted to assuage her mother's suffering by giving her company for which she will have to sacrifice her future. What was the necessity of her all those studies if that was the final thing that was stored in her destiny? Was that not a total waste? The education she had completed, the knowledge she earned, all would be simply waste if she could not utilize them for the benefit of the people?

She had no answers for all these questions. She did not know if God had any. He must have sent the problems to try them. He was carefully carrying, his plan forward. She left everything to God.

(17)

Love and compassion are necessities not luxuries, without them humanity cannot survive

-   Dalai Lama

Dr. Anjan Saikia had already secured a job and joined at Nijaraghuli Public Health Centre which was quite far from Guwahati. For a boy born and brought up in Guwahati, a place like Nijaraghuli was a sort of punishment posting. Not to speak of any cinema hall, there was not even a proper tea stall to sit and relax. Anjan thought that he will definitely suffer from boredom.

Anjan had to go Shillong for his pay authority ship, so he came to Guwahati after about two months. One full day was necessary to collect the pay authority ship from the Accountant General's office in Shillong. So Anjan made a plan to take Nandita also to Shillong so that they could spend a good time together there. Nandita was also in great sorrow for the loss of her father, so she would be able to ease off her stress she had been suffering. Nandita liked the idea and gladly consented.

Getting down from at the Shillong bus stand they went straight to the AG Office where Anjan submitted his papers and requested the concerned person to process. The concerned dealing assistant advised Anjan to come in the late afternoon to collect the pay slip. Then they went to a hotel nearby to spend the time.

Nandita was initially a bit shaky to stay inside a room with Anjan. But at the same time she did not just want to loiter around aimlessly. Anjan assured her to relax and to remain in her normal self. After some description of that God forsaken place Nandita divereted the topic to the sad demise of her father. Nandita moisted her lips and said 'The loss of my father is a giant blow to me. He was the pillar of strength of my life and I couldn't pass a single day without thinking of him. I miss him badly.'

Anjan's arm crept around her shoulder and said softly 'Console yourself with the thought that you did your best.'

'That again pricked my conscience. We couldn't do anything. We just left him at Gods mercy, and now I suffer from unending repentance. The memory of that day will haunt me for life.'

To ease her sorrow, Anjan hoped to romanticize the atmosphere and stroked her hair and then moved his hand over her back. Nandita did not object and she was passively gazing though the window and felt Anjan's amorous advances. Anjan took her in arms and kissed her ardently which was more sensuous than tender. She enjoyed his alluring affectionate moves. Her breathe shortened. She smiled as though she were comforted by Anjan's warm embrace like giant worm. He said obsequiously 'All is fair in love and war.'

Anjan gave a deep kiss on her lips. Nandita reciprocated with kiss on his both cheeks. Both were stung by the arrows of love. Then she kissed him on the lips. They were licking each others lips gently for a along time. He took her to the bed. Nandita felt hypnolized and slowly slowly she undressed herself and surrendered to Anjan. Anjan was inpatient and was engaged in act of love making. Nandita closed her eyes and went a long with the proceedings. They cuddled up together under the blanket and were madly in love making.

After their a whirl wind romance they laid silently and didn't talk to each other for quite sometime. Nandita was moving her hand over the hairy chest of Anjan. There was a look of contrite on her face. She asked 'I become unchaste for the first time. Is it a sin committed by us?'

Anjan gave a delighted smile 'It was all innocent fun. We will be married soon. Nobody on earth could be able to separate us.

Anjan cupped her face with hands and he kissed her chastely on her cheeks. Nandita moved her finger through the hair of Anjan and said 'You are leaving for Nijaraghuli and you will be busy there. You will meet many new people, your job also is a challenging one. Please don't take it otherwise will your attraction to me wane or fade out?'

'How could you imagine such kind of ridiculous thing. You are my love of life. My love to you is free from lust. I hate flirting.'

Nandita got down from the bed and started collecting her dresses. 'No' Nandita gave a wicked grin. She was putting one leg inside her salwar. 'I didn't mean that. I wanted to know will you not miss me? People say 'Out of sight is out of mind.'

'Ofcourse not' Anjan looked her fondly and said 'You will also be there with me emotionally. Certainly I will miss you much. There is another saying 'Absence makes the heart grow fonder.'

Anjan took her hand by the hand and he looked at her and smile. He took out his wallet from the pocket and delved for something. Nandita gazed with amusement. Anjan pulled her ring finger and slided the gold ring with a genial smile.

Nandita embraced him warmly. Nandita sat on the sofa. 'When are you coming back again? I will feel lonely. I will miss you very much.'

'Maximum after two months'. He tied his belt and dropped in the sofa. He said 'I will then go to Barsila to meet your mother to place my formal proposal for our marriage. My parents are anxious to get the thing wrapped up early.'

We are only puppets, our strings are being pulled by some unknown force. We don't have control of our situations which suddenly takes abrupt change. The romantic atmosphere inside the room quickly turned into a depressingly gloomy one.

Nandita was stuck by the sudden thought of her mother. How her mother would react to the proposal? She was a withdrawn person after the death of her husband and was not interested in any affairs of the children. Nandita thought how happy she would have been if her father were alive. Water gathered in her eyes. Nandita said in a low voice. 'My mother is leading a life of recluse and she is surviving at the mercy of domestic help Tara.'

She again said wiping her eyes 'Both my parents would have been extremely happy but...'

Anjan put his index finger over her lips to stop her from sad topic.

'Anjan I am constantly disturbed how will she carry on living alone? She will spend her nights only to wait for the sun to reappear.' Her face wore a puzzled look.

'What to do?' Anjan sighed a deep breathe and shook his head tiredly.

Nandita was in a deep agony. She said 'Can we not do anything for correcting the situation to allerate their discomfort by giving them company, by providing them a little comfort during in their old days? Can we save them from their feelings of being redundant like what we did to Madhabi?'

Anjan's romantic mood drifted away and turned serious. He preferred to keep mum and listened to Nandita's emotional monologue.

'Well Anjan tell me one thing' She said looking straight to Anjan 'Should we live for ourself. Is it a success, amassing lot of wealth, garner all material comfort, keeping our parents ignored at fag end of their life? How can people be so much self centred? Did conscience not prick us when we see the suffering of others both physically and mentally? Can we just ignore our feelings? Specially when it happens to some one very close to our heart?'

All the romantic feelings of Anjan disappeared in the air. Anjan stony faced and said 'So far as I understand we are all bound by the cycle of life. Every individuals must try to achieve success.' Anjan looked outside and said in an authoritative tone 'To establish ourselves in the society is the success. This is the tradition of human history. It is not correct to denounce individual success as selfishness.'

'What about our society?' Nandita intercepted quickly. 'About the poor and weak people around us? For whom the basic needs like food, health care and shelter are limited? Don't we have any responsibly towards them? Can we be happy by turning blind eye on them and live in isolation? Why then people yearn for a society? Is it not a propensity for self denial?'

'We must walk in the path the society had laid down for us. We are doctors and we have a defined role in the society. We must render selfless service in health care sector without any discrimination rich or poor. That is our commitment to the society and society wants the same from us.'

Nandita was uncomprehending. Her question was basically about the sufferings of loneliness of people who are helpless who don't have support, physical and financial, whose daily struggle are to fight with utter desolation. They silently await for the death. A pathetic life. For them destiny is the ultimate word.' She did not get answer for all these questions.

'Look' Anjan laid his hand on her and nodded sagely. 'How can we take all the responsibility? Where is our scope? There are designated people in the society to take care of various issues. It is not proper to think that we will have to look after every issue.'

They exclanged their views for a couple of minutes. Anjan moved his hand in affection. He sat besides her touching her body. Anjan was not sure whether she liked that. She was looking vacuously through the window in a pensive mood.

'Anjan'. Nandita spoke with composed voice 'I am confused. If I join service I may not be posted in same place which may be far from your place of posting. Then how frequently I will be able to meet you or my sickly helpless mother?'

Anjan nodded his head and whispered in her ear. 'You have to find out a suitable mix of your life and your parent's family. People are managing like this only.' He gave a pause. He was in vexation and was not sure whether Nandita paid any heed to what he was saying. He teased 'Do you want to float in air with elusive ideas by denying the progressive outlook of human civilization. Any way do you have an inkling of becoming a hermit.' After a little pause Don't get upset I was only teasing.'

Nandita didn't like the snide remarks of Anjan. Anjan looked remorse. He repented of his act which obviously hurt her sentiment.

Nandita thought that Anjan was right that the general perspective of people is that a girl wants company of handsome competent man who can assure emotional security and comfort. Man and wife are complementary to each other. People normally don't think beyond that. Nandita felt that our material needs had caused irreparable damage to moral values.

Nandita debated with herself for a while. Finally love over powered those feeble disagreements. Anjan kissed her with emotion. She did not object.

'At some point of time people think of doing something great' Anjan said putting his hand over her shoulder and said in a soothing voice 'Night time fancies that disappear in the morning. People become matured and realistic and they discard those utopian fantasy. We must first get established or else society either don't trust or accept.'

(18)

Love is the only force capable of transforming an enemy into a friend

-   *Martin Luther King Jr.*

Malabika was amused to see the collection of sand, brick and cheaps in front of her father's house. Conventionally that was the time for Barua to wash his hands from new construction activities. Was there any need? Who will stay there? Actually an engineer's psyche revolves only within the periphery of civil construction. They don't find their utility if they don't engage themselves in construction works. He wanted to utilize his knowledge to the fullest extent. As if he was the epitome of building construction.

Malabika failed to understand why at the fag end of their life they need extension of house. To her these were wasteful expenditures. Nobody can take the property with him after death. They should save money for urgent necessity like treatment or for any such exigency. They need enough money to live in comfort in their old age. Prospects of earning rent was also very remote in place like Maniktola. She was unable to hide her curiosity and asked her father. 'Deuta are you going for some construction like extension of the house? But why?'

'Yes' Barua rubbed his palms and smiled obsequiously and said 'Planning something like that to make myself busy. We should remain busy else disease will attack and try to intrude into our bodies. Boredom shortens the life. Land also need to the utilized, so that constant maintenance could be avoided. The yard is overgrown with wild grasses which need regular trimming.'

Malabika nodded in agreements though she was not fully convinced by the explanation. It is possible to draw a parallel between age and sentiment. More over she was aware about her father's arrogance. She preferred not to take the debate any further and to leave him to do whatever he liked. 'Why should I interfere?' She shrugged off and murmured to herself.

In reality Barua had a different strategy altogether. They were getting old and naturally they wanted somebody to look after them. They have none other than Malabika. Only daughter and son in law were staying in a rented house in the same town was considered by them as awkward. Barua and his wife had already buried all their bitterness. They wanted to heal the old wound fast. Already the sourness of their relationship disappeared after reconciliation from both sides. So much so that Barua's family was very much fond of Banibrata. They therefore wanted to bring their daughter and son in law nearer to them. Hence Barua indented to make an extension of their house to create additional accommodation for them. After all they are the sole heir of all the properties possessed by Barua. But he hesitated to reveal his intension because it was delicate and had some intrinsic complexity. The proposal might hurt Banibrata's self esteem. So the best course of action was to wait for the opportune moment. Time alone will tell.

Never the less Mala's mother took the lead. One day when Mala came from college to her parent's house in the afternoon her mother disclosed the proposal and said very politely. 'Mala we are adding to ages and this or that disease comes to us.' Mother said to Malabika with compassion 'You are in a rented house. Both of you can stay with us and give us company. Forgot about the word law, he is our son now' She chuckled in delight.

Malabika kept quiet for sometime. There was some sense in her words. Mrs. Barua broke the silence and said again 'We have nobody to look after. After one of us leave this world, you are the only person to depend upon. As the day passes we are scared for our old age ailments. I am already suffering from diabetic complications and your father is a hypertension patient. Everything is uncertain in the midst of certainity.'

Malabika was emotionally swayed. She interrupted 'Why you again raised these evil thoughts.' She laid her hand on mothers hand and said 'Let's see what happens in time. But as on today you are quite strong and active. It will not be advisable to come and intrude into your domain and adversely affect your privacy. Two's a company three's a crowd. To many people staying together leads to unpleasantness and the relations get sour. More over such a proposal may hurt the self respect of Banibrata.'

'What privacy is there left for us now?' Mother said in a reticent tone 'Your happiness is all we yearn to see. I do not envisage that he should mind this arrangement, In fact it will be mutually advantageous.'

Malabika gazed outside and saw the masion and helpers working attentively. She was amused to watch how time changes the world. That once a swindler, son of a wretched school teacher got converted into an adorable son now. How all these bitter feelings vanished in course of time? Time is the best healer. Actually time is the solution of every problem.

'Alright. We will think over the proposal and take a decision at the appropriate time. Now let the house be completed and father's wish be fulfilled.' Malabika quickly wrapped up the discussion.

The proposal sounded to be ridiculous at first sight to both Banibrata. He was man of self respect and that was his major concern. A man who lives in his father-in-laws family is looked down in the society. He started his life from scratch. So he did not like to succumb to others grace and to bring disrepute to his self esteem. Moreover his conscience pricked that his mother was languishing alone in a place without dependable help. Would it be justified for him to take refuse in the in-laws house? How the society would react to such an indecorous action?

Malabika however had forgiven her parents for all their disgusting and crude behaviour of past. After all they were her parents. There was no point in keeping them lonely specially at their advance age. They have nobody except their only child, to whom they had to fall back as a support.

Malabika had a little bit of inclination to accept the offer with some mutually agreed terms. They would have their kitchen separate. They should have their independent entries. Nobody should raise questions about their respective guests. They would be staying adjacently but not together.

All said and done finally Banibrata and Malabika shifted to the newly extended part of Barua's main house. All opposition to Banibrata and Malabika's love affairs, all the initial unpleasantness and bitterness about their marriage had ended like a film story. The turbulence ran over the family for paste couple of months pacified and normallcy to both families was happily restored.

Nandita since quite some time was in an indecisive battle. She was confused about her future. Marriage with Anjan and to join in profession were apparently the option before her under the common perception.. Thoughts of her mother's loneliness persistently whirled around in her mind.

Few days back Nandita went home and wanted to spend some time with her mother. She was extremely sad to find her mother dolefully reticent. Nilima Kakati almost refuse talking with people. She preferred aloofness and solitude. A mood of melancholy descended over the house. Nandita was stifling in the lifeless house. How her mother will live in such a ghastly gloomy situation? Her mind was fastened with those depressing feelings. Nandita was restless in trying to unravel the tangled thoughts.

Banibrata and Malabika invited Nandita to come and stay with them for a break. Nandita was also eager to go to Maniktola to meet her elder brother and sister in law. They were very fond of her.

It was a pleasant autumn evening, Mild cold air shook the town. Dry leaves were strewn in the outside courtyard. Both Malabika and Nandita sat side by side in their front varandah and exchanged general conversation.

Malabika turned to Nandita and said courteously 'Nandita' She looked straight to her eyes. 'You are now a qualified doctor. It's a very laborious and expensive education and also a very noble profession. Society look doctors with great reverence. For a patient doctors are next to God. Obviously there is lot of expectations of the society from a doctor that too a lady doctor is much more special.'

Nandita did not respond hastily because she was not sure what Malabika was hinting at. Certainly she was not discussing the nobility of the profession. Malabika again said 'What is your next plan? Which is your priority service study or marriage?'

'Bou' Nandita threw her vision outside. 'I am in a fix and unable to decide anything. Should I persue higher studies in specialised. discipline or I should start working forthwith?'

'What about the marriage? Anjan must be eagerly awaiting.'

Nandita evaded the question of marriage. She said 'He has already joined in service. He is coming to Guwahati on a break for couple of days later. To my mind Anjan has done the right thing. In our rural society necessity of a general practitioner is more suitable than a specialist.'

Till then Banibrata did not join the conversation. He was listening to Nandita heedfully and then said 'So you may also find a job in a health department and start your career as a doctor. You will be able to serve the poor and needy people and do justice to your noble profession.'

'Yes'. Nandita's expression turned excited. Some beautiful thought peeped into her mind. 'All those rural areas are similar to our Barsila. I can opt to serve our own people at Barsila.'

'Barsila?' Banibrata interrupted like a bullet and said 'Barsila doesn't have necessary infrastructure, diagnostic lab or pharmacy. It is an under staffed primary health centre without any modern laboratory and imaging equipments. Moreover one doctor is already serving there. You should try for some better posting, so that you can gain better experience.

'Yes'. A glean of light beam flashed in her mind and she replied with composure. 'It's much better to serve my own people. Moreover I will be able to lessen the remorsefulness of my mother.' Colours flooded her face when she thought of that. At that moment she was not worried about money and instead she was feeling some contentment in dreaming her service to the needy and helpless people of her village. 'I know there are lot of problems. Still I will surely get solace in serving hundreds of Madhabis and lots of lonely ailing old people. I have deeply considered all aspects and gathered an urge to serve our deprived people. However I need sometime to mull it over before making a decision.'

Malabika thought of side tracking the topic of discussion. She looked at Nandita quizzically and raised question over and again. 'And what about your marriage?'

There was a tense silence for a while. Nandita's expression grew solemn. She thought all these matters are premature. But perhaps she was not right. Her age could not wait indefinitely. Malabika was rightfully interested to know the things that was in her mind.

'Bou' she glanced gloomily at Malabika and said 'Can you imagine any body not to speak of a doctor, will come forward to work with me in a substandard health care centre leaving a lucrative luxurious life. It is highly improbable to get a person like that. So let me set out the sail alone steering through the freezing fog.'

Nandita's thoughts were in disarray. She was frantically trying to find answer to the dilemas she had encountered with.

Their impression of Nandita was sharply changed as if they had never knew her truly. They thought she was a jovial and romantic girl by temperament. Banibrata and Malabika attempted for a sleep. But sleep drifted away from them. Might be Nandita was also devoid of a good sleep.

Nandita needed time to defuse her stresses of mind with a good sleep. She recollected the saying of Victor Hugo 'A mother's arms are made of tenderness and children sleep soundly in them.' She visualized that she was in a deep sea and her mother beckoned her over the waves.

(19)

Ever has it been that loves knows not its own death until the hour of separation

- *Khalil Gibran*

Harsh winter is very short in Guwahati. Perhaps it lasts only for a few days utmost. It was one of such cold days. Light breeze was blowing. Nandita went out with heavy warm clothes. The days are short. It was almost dark. Fireflies were dancing with sparkled lights both sides of the hostel approach road. After about two months Anjan had come to Guwahati.

As already planned Anjan was waiting at the specified point. Both of them boarded into an auto rickshaw and proceeded towards Fancy bazar. They were feeling chilly due the cold breeze hitting them. They didn't talk in presence of the auto driver. Both were infact reminiscing what to talk and how to start? The presence of the third person made the silence as blessings in disguise.

They entered a restaurant and sat in a table for four by the window overlooking the snarled traffic on the street. Both of them were trying to unravel the skein of the tangled thought which were winding in their mind. Anjan broke the silence and led the conversation. 'I am leaving for Nijaraghuli next Sunday that means only after two days hence. This time I had planned to stay for a longer period.

Nandita didn't react as if she turned a deaf ear to what he was saying. She sat in silence. Doubts were whirling on her head. She was trying to string the words together. Anjan looked pale and sullen. He pretended as if he was carefully studying the menu card.

'Well Anjan' Nandita gave him a blank gaze. 'My mother is so lonely that I feel totally dejected and I have almost lost interest in doing anything. She has completely withdrawn from everything. She is more melancholic than she had been and so more quiet. She is perhaps totally disappointed at the way that all her near and dear one are gradually going away from her. She had not been able to come to termus with her immanent loneliness. I am afraid she might fall into severe depression.'

'It is sad. She had to stay like that. But that is the law of nature.' Anjan said casually.

'I know you don't appreciate such feelings. But can you imagine that I should leave her like that?' She didn't say 'abandon' though she meant that in her heart. 'We will enjoy life and let her suffer in depression.' Is it not a deliberate disregard to leave a helpless person who has nothing but gloom and despondency?'

Anjan opted to stay away from contentious topic. He believed that she would be relieved of her anxiety after venting out her thoughts.

Nandita said after a pause 'The loss of my father was the most traumatic event in my life. I can't forget the pain. We could not do anything. What is the meaning of our life if we can't be of their help when needed most?'

'I don't understand Nandita why are you so much mixed up in these thoughts? What are you trying to do? Everybody cares for the family, for the parents. We can try to support them, help them but the result is not in our hand. This is the tradition society is following. Puzzling about these thoughts are waste of time.' He said bluntly risking displeasure from Nandita.

'And our society?' Nandita looked unhappy and was gnawing her finger nails. 'The sufferings of the people around us? They don't mean anything to us? Should we not work to alleviate the sufferings of our own people?'

'Yes we will have to provide them necessary treatment, honestly and sincerely.' Anjan said lightly. 'We have to follow the tradition. In fact society precisely expect that from us. Government have made us doctors by spending money and now we should render service to the people in return.' Anjan said the words persuasively.

Nandita was wrapping her thoughts and looked at Anjan with disapproval.

'We are doctors. Our ethic is to provide treatment to the patients without any discrimination. That is our commitment to the society'. He took a pause, looked through the window and said. More over we should raise a family through which we will pass on the responsibility to the next generation. Life is a circle. The end of one journey is the beginning of the next. There is a rhythm of life that everything moves in perfect symphony with others.'

Sudden coolness shivered through Nandita. She was worried stiff. She seemed outwardly composed, but was annoyed. 'But what about those who have no able person to look after, those who do not get access to modern health care. They are still depend upon fate and superstition. For whom luck is the last refuse. They hopelessly waited for their impending death accompanying pain.'

Anjan tried to make out what Nandita was hinting out. He thought not to extend the arguments. He had no answer to her puzzling thoughts as such, which were reeling again in vicious circle. Anjan laid her hands with affection and pressed to show his bondness. He was not sure of her reaction, encouragement or dejection.

'Anjan' She asked curiously 'What you want from me? I should join a job? To accumulate material comfort?' To give birth to children to educate them to take care of the family' You want me to show others how a good wife should be and boast among your firends?'

'Yes, exactly true' Anjan was about to say in jubilation but he hold back and said diligently. 'To some extent true. Everybody wants a prosperous happy comfortable life and whoever has achieved, they are respected in the society as a successful person'.

Nandita had a wicked glint in her eyes and felt a trace of sarcasm in the quizzical remark of Anjan. Silence prevailed for unusually long time. A note of discord an dissatisfaction echoed in her mind. She was gulping her thought inside. 'Yes to make the family life happy, wife has a very important role. Any young girl yearns for a capable handsome man as husband. Husband and wife are complimentary to each other. But apart from this this conventional concept can woman play some other role?'

Anjan touched her hand and pressed it. Crack appeared in their relations progressively got widened. Their conceptions of happiness stood poles apart. Nandita was convinced that marriage and raising a family could not be the sole objective in woman's life. She was by then determined to stay away from the traditional path which according to Anjan and for many others was not worthy and practical.

'Are you sure that looking after the family, giving birth to children, taking care of all of you, I get the fulfilment of success which you term as the peak of happiness?' Nandita said fixing her stare at Anjan.

Anjan hold her hand 'My emotional and financial support will be always for you. We will inspire each other to achieve success in life, and try to be happy, right?'

'What the parents get after the success of their children'. Her tone was curt and unfriendly 'I believe you have seriously missed the bonding, compassion and sympathy part of life. Selfishness in the long run.' She shook her head in disapproval.

'Success of the children is the top most priority for the parents. They suffer and sacrifice to ensure their triumph in this competitive world. At the end of the day that is their contentment.'

Anjan noticed that reconciliation of their differences appeared dim. Anjan felt that thoughts warded off an another tack. She looked pensive and said 'There is serious differences between you and me. I have reasons to believe that we may not be able to get along throughout this long journey of life ahead. Perdon me my mind is utterly disturbed. You may not be able to perceive my views clearly.'

Anjan was visibly shocked. His face turned white as bones. He knew without a shadow of doubt that she was signalling an imminent breakup. A relationship of three years. Can that be broken in a momentary pressure? Hoping against hope he had a belief that once her emotional trauma dissipate she would be back to normal again.

Suddenly Nandita started fidgeting in her chair. She collected her bag and stood up. She released a long breathe. 'Alright, I have made up my mind.' She wiped a tear from her eyes and murmured. 'Eventually my decision is immutable and please don't try to infringe into that. I will go back to my village. I think I will have to rescind my decision for marriage. Please forgive me.'

Anjan was horrified and stunned. After a spell of silence he despairingly said 'Self abnegated decision? I think your idealistic philosophy may not last long. Grass is greener on the other side of the fence.' He shook his head and said 'Alright I will wait till your flight of fancy fade away from your mind. One thing you might have missed the point that people need money to serve others. Anyway do not linger your experiment with life and waste time. Time and tide wait for none.' Anjan looked dejected 'Of course right or wrong is absolutely your decision. I presume I have already lost any right to advice you.' Anjan and Nandita eye each other wearily.

Instead of being frightened Anjan's discouraging remarks infused more courage in her. She became more stubborn and confident. Like a flicker back into the flame 'Sorry' She mumbled. Some thing had emerged inside her. They stood facing each other at the tresold of the restaurant. She whimpered 'I will go to Barsila tomorrow. I think we will not meet again. May be God willing we meet in our lifetime someday somewhere. May God be with you.?'

Anjan didn't say anything. He felt as though his hopes were just shattered like a piece of glass. He was surprised to see a glow in her face. Sun was creasing in the horizon. The orange coloured beam of sun light brightened her cheeks. Anjan dulled himself consciously against the shock. He could not believe how easily they could broke up.

Coming out from the restaurant they took a few steps in opposite directions. In a moment Nandita turned and call for Anjan. She was hiding her auxiety and pull the ring out from her finger and cooly handed it over to him. She said ' I bid you adieu'.

The poignancy of parting and separation broke Anjan to tears. In a short time she disappeared behind a crowd. Anjan could not see her anymore. Sudden emptiness appalled him and water welled up in his eyes.

Anjan walked aimlessly and reached the bank of Dighali tank. The rippling of wave glinted in the moonlight. A fear of abandonment inflicted upon him, feeling of severing of their relations. He stood absolutely motionless. He felt as if he hit the end of the world. Dark clouds gathered in the sky meant a rain was coming. He was unmindful. He was not in hurry to go home. It was like a dream that one little conversation led to an irrevocable split up. The dream overturned.

(20)

**Through selfless service you will always be fruitful and find the
fulfilment of your desire..**

- *Bhagavat Geeta*

Nandita moved to her home at Barsila for good. To return back to her native place was the most agonizing decision of her life. She sacrified the normal easy prospects and choose the struggle. The Royal Poinciana (Krishna Chura) tree near their house was looking awesome with flowers of fire. The graceful Mesua ferrea (Nahar) near the gate chooped beautiful pink leaves and fragrant white flowers. Nandita's mind glow with sheer desperation to devote herself on a altruistic mission to help the poor and needy villagers with a view to alleviate their sufferings and loneliness. Neither she had any past experience nor any financial back up but her strength was indomitable determination and focuss for her vision. She tried to discuss her plan with her mother who obviously didn't have anything to bolster her confidence. Nilima Kakati was ostensibly happy, which didn't escaped Nandita's notice. She had undeniable anxiety for Nandita's future. Undernealth her cool exterior, she was disappointed that Nandita had eschwed the social customs of a girl's life.

Nandita converted her bed room and renovated the same to make it her clinic and she shifted herself to her mother's room. She started with a modest beginning by offering treatment at a nominal fee. Gradually the people came to know about the functioning of the clinic and patients started pouring in. Setting up a Health Care Centre cropped up in her mind.

Nandita throughout her life could not brush aside her ignominy of the sufferings of young Madhabi who finally had to succumb to her illness without any treatment. She was the allegorical figure of the perilous inadequacy of health care in the locality. So she named her clinic as 'Madhabi Health Care Centre, 'Madhabi Swastha

Sewa Kendra,' which was very basic in nature. People were however full of enthusiasm which emboldened her in putting more effort in pursuing the aim of providing proper advice, initial treatment and emotional support to sick and lonely persons of the society. She was aware that the task ahead was stupendous but the source of strength was the undeterred support of the people.

Naming of a house was till then was not popular among the residents of Barsila because almost, everyone knew each other. Moreover Gobinda Kakati needed no introduction. People referred his name with deep revegence. All members of the family were idolised by people of Barsila. Hence a plaque in front of his house was unconceivable. People's curiosity arosed when they noticed the mysterious name plate in front of the centre. Naming of a house in the cities and bigger towns were seen seldom. The common names were 'Kamalaya', 'Gourisadan' 'Kalpa kutir', which were named to commernorate their father or mother or in the devotion to God. Thus people were astonished to see the name "Madhabi Swastha Sewa Kendra,' People therefore were inquisitive about the name. Madhabi Swastha Sewa Kendra. Dr. Nandita has setup the health centre in a makeshift shed on the vacant piece of land in a bamboo walled room, inside their compound with support and initiative from Banibrata. He requested local villagers to donate some bamboo and people were more than eager to support them. The local boys constructed the shed almost free. A local hardware goods dealer donated a few C.1. sheets and the shed was ready for the purpose. She recruited girls and trained them in basic nursing job and also some boys to assist her.

During the course of her treatment she came across a few number of people who needed nursing and care but those were not available in their home for obvious reason. The people are poor and ignorant. So a new idea came to her mind. 'Why not one or two such type of women patients are provided with accommodation there in her centre?' She foresaw that her mother would also be able to meet other women and spend some time talking with them. Nandita made her chamber at one end and the rest part she kept reserved to accommodate the patients and old inmates. Medicine suppliers generously donated medicines double the amount sought for by Nandita. In turn she used to give medicines free besides the food to the boarders.

Initially a very few people came there. People looked highly sceptical about the success of the venture. Some people even doubt her capability. How come a qualified doctor could attempt such a gamble sacrificing a promising career? How long she could sustain by rendering free service? Where from she would meet up the expenses? Some people again ridiculed her mission as a freak of fantasy.

But Nandita was staunchly steadfast in her determination to face any challenges. She was intensely focused not to let challenges dispirit her. It had taken sometime to earn the trust of the people. Gradually the Madhabi health care centre flourished in manifold. There had been a great deal of publicity in the nearby area about the activities of the centre. The local reporters flocked to the centre to collect information for preparing their news stories.

'Madam, What this name means? What is the significance of this name?'

'Madhabi was a young girl hailed from a neighbouring village.' She replied with her usual composer. 'Her father was impoverished peasant and could not maintain his family. He felt relieved by keeping her in our house as maid servant. Her actual name was Nandita. She had to sacrifice her name for the shake of living. My father changed her name because that was same as mine. So that poor Nandita vanished here and Madhabi was born. After a couple years he was suffering from a terminal disease and she had to be sent back to her village. She left her sobriquet Madhabi here. She was deprived of modern health care facilities and had to succumb to death without proper treatment Madhabi epitomised the suffering of the people because of their poverty and deprivation.' This health care centre is named in commemoration of Madhabi who is no more today.'

'What is the purpose of this centre?' The reporters asked critically.

'See, there is complete lack of awareness about the modern medical treatment among the people.' Nandita asserted 'Our primary objective is to provide basic modern health care and also to advice the proper follow up treatment. to the poor and needy people in order to dissuade people from the clutch of superstitions, quackery and sorcery healing practices. We treat them and refer them for further treatment where better facilities are available. We propose to provide facilities at a bare minimum cost as far as possible.'

'Do you have any plan to keep indoor patients here in future?' Someone from behind asked her.

'Yes' Nandita wiped her spectacles to clean them and said 'I have already started in an experimental basis. I am hopeful and have an idea to extend the mission a step further. To give relief the people who suffer from acute loneliness and nobody is there to look after them at the fag end of their life. They need our empathy. Our society is slowly swayed towards westernised way of living. Old parents are suffering from melancholy due to acute loneliness. The sense of redundancy is escalating among the old parents. The houses are becoming the empty nest.' She said with humiliation. 'They need emotional support, our sympathy and care. Though I have this mission yet I humbly admit that these are tall wishes. Let us see to what extent we can accomplish.'

The news of Madhabi Swastha Sewa Kendra with her photograph was published in several leading news papers. People from far distant places had started visiting her project. Benevolent people impressed by her mission approached Nandita for help and donations. Money and materials started pouring and gradually permanent structures came up in the centre. She recruited nursing staff and installed primary diagnostic equipments. She made arrangements for inpatients at a nominal cost to meet up the expenses for food and disposable materials. Generous people business houses and institutions besides cash donated in the form of food equipments, furniture's and medicines regularly, There were people who were far too pessimistic looking dark side of the things. She disliked to respond to their sneering comments.

'You have no modern equipments, how can you make proper diagnostic assessments?'

'Yes', She tried to control her emotion and said calmly. 'I know, but as a qualified doctor I can make the basic diagnosis of the disease and advice for future course of treatment. Presently our activities will be to provide primary health care and to create awareness of modern treatment, to provide shelter and emotional security to the needy older people suffering from loneliness.'

With the passing of time Nandita's selfless service shamed all her critics. Dr. Nandita was showered with profuse appreciation by the people far and wide. Large business houses and companies came up with support for infrastructure building, ambulance etc. to Madhabi Swastha Sewa Kendra. Government's assistances also started pouring in for assets creation and extension of the centre. Local people came to render voluntary service to the Kendra.

Step by step Madhabi Swastha Sewa Kendra flourished and became a renowned institution in the state. Nandita purchased plot of nearby land and new buildings were erected there. The institution grew like a full fledged old age home with inbuilt basic medical facilities.

Banibrata and Malabika frequently visited the centre. Perhaps they looked with pride by watching Nandita in landing at the rainbow in her dream. However if anybody was immensely benefitted it was Nilima Kakati. Her mental and physical weakness all got substancially reduced. She spent most of her time with the inmates who were of her age. For her that was always a blissful time of the day. She was relieved of her loneliness and despair to a great extent.

In the initial stage Nilima Kakati discouraged Nandita and said, 'You have become a qualified doctor, first lady doctor of Barsila. We want you to take up the professional career. Me and your father had a longing to see your marriage. But he was fortunate that he left us before.' She looked sorrowful.

Nandita sighed and a mood of melancholy descended on her. As a mother it was quite natural for her to be concerned with the future of her daughter. She earnestly yearn to see Nandita married and established. Nandita's activities had initially disappointed her. She was stuck by the incongruity of the situation. Eventually she could not enforce her vision upon Nandita and finally withdrawn from thinking on the subject. She resigned and accepted that destiny had a separate plan for Nandita and she had to pursue that. These were past but still echoed sometime in the mind of Nandita. Now Nilima Kakati had found many reasons to be happy with the activities of Nandita.

A few incidents were stamped indelibly in Nandita's memory. The first day when in patient came for treatment. The day when the first microscope reached her centre. She got a telephone connection and then the ambulance. Then several items and equipments reached there. The centre was gleaming with every joyful incidents. Nandita acknowledged all such help and support with her usual humility. The premise of her centre was used by outside agencies and organisations for demonstration of selfless social service. Her health care centre was referred as icon in the society among the new generation to learn to dream for the rainbow in their heart.

The accounting of the centre was meticulously maintained and was fully transparent. Nandita also was one among the employees in the organisation at pay role. They were paid very nominal remunerations. Food was same for all excepting the sick and the old women whose diets were prepared as per suitability of their health conditions. The centre was running in a no profit no loss basis. In case some surplus money got accrued the same were used to acquire additional items to improve the living conditions of the inmates.

Nandita was greatly encouraged by the wonderful response and the unstinting support of the people. She found the purpose of living in her project. The work had kept her captivated for last few years. She devoted her full energy and time among the patients, among the people suffering from old age ailments and loneliness. She had a very large extended family in the patients, employees and well wishers. However occasionally past memories haunted her and made her gloomy. The saying of William Shakespeare 'It is not in the star to hold our destiny but in ourselves' was her satisfaction.

(21)

Our gratest glory is not in never failing, but in rising every time we fall

- *Confucious*

Nijaraghuli was a small semi urban town situated about hundred miles away from Guwahati. Regular bus service was available from the Guwahati to the sub divisional headquarter nearest to Nijaraghuli. The remaining portion was connected by a gravel road and there was no proper mode of transport. People commute mainly by jeep or truck fron Nijaraghuli to the nearest town.

It had a high school, a post office, one paddy husk mill, a few shops and recently setup primary health centre where Dr. Anjan Saikia joined as the first medical officer. Till his arrival the compounder was running the show authoritatively.

There was a big poud and people used to swim, wash clothes, catch fish and also drink water from there. Resultantly the people were mostly suffering from water borne disease and the health centre use to give carminative mixures to cure the gastro related diseases. Thus the compounder was infact very popular among the residents of that sleepy town.

Arrival of a doctor was therefore not a very welcoming news to the compounder and his admirers. But after coming in contact with Anjan the people gradually shifted their loyality to him, which was mostly because of his graceful dealings, soothing and courtesious dealings with the patients.

Nijaraghuli was a very small place specially for a person of multifeed quality like Anjan. There was hardly anybody with whom he could make friendship. Slowly however he started mixing with one or two school teachers and an owner of book stall.

They used to talk about various subjects related to disease, music, women. They spent times by playing cards. Anjan could adjust well in the area and was more or less happy.

One day one young boy around twelve years was brought to the dispensary with complain of intermittent fever. He had been suffering since last four days.

Anjan initially suspected malaria but the disease took a turn to pneumonia. Anjan was trying his best to contain his disease but exact medicines were not available there at that moment. He asked the family to procure the medicines from the sub-divisional head quarter or to take the patient to Guwahati. As ill luck would have it the family also could not assess the gravity of the ailment and the boy breathed his last after three days in hospital. The entire blame be fell on Anjan and he was made responsible for everything that went wrong because he was treating him.

Incidentally the boy was the only male child to his parents. More over the boy's father was the owner of the rice mill and was the richest business man in the town and he commanded wide influence over the residents. So instead of being sad they became infuriated more and they all started blaming Anjan for wrong treatment. A group of unruly people burst into the dispensary. The gathering hurled slang and abusive words to Anjan who was hiding inside his quarter. The angry mob turned violent and ransacked his quarter. He was physically assaulted he was knocked down. He was injured and he had several bruises in his body.

The compounder who till other day was the nameshake doctor added fuel to the flame. Anjan bowed to the nob and begged for mercy and finally the mob dispersed after causing extensive damage to his belonging besides his reputation. None of his friends bothered to come to help him. The incident made Anjan extremely frightened, because for no fault of his he had to face the irks of the people.

Government had set up the health centre without adequate medicines or staffs. In fact some useless mediciues required for heart patients were dumped in the centre in abundance. Somebody in the helm of affairs might have purchased huge quantity of unnecessary medicines taking some cut money and distributed to these centres. Anjan did not ruled out the possible conspirational aspect of the compounder. Because Anjan's presence had affected his practice and source of earning.

After careful thought of all pros and cons for the whole night Anjan decided to leave the place and seek transfer to somewhere else. He groped his way in the wee hours of night and started walking stealthily to run away from there. It was still dark and he came out boldly into the darkness. Lanters twinkled here and there in the nearby village. He headed out on foot under the cover of darkness with a slight hunch as though cringing a tad at thought of somebody noticing. Nobody was on the road excepting a few way laid dogs stared and whined at him mysteriously. Mild barkings broke the silence of the sleepy night like dropping of pebbles in the pond. Anjan moved half running and looked around wildly. The dogs were perhaps confirmed that the stranger was not a thief or even if they were not responsible for anybody's property. He sweated with friht due to unknown danger lurking in the darkness around.

After an hour or so he crossed the area of Nijaraghuli he took some rest in an expression of great relief. Suddenly he saw a mini truck coming to wards him. He stopped it and pleaded for lift. The truck was bound for Guwahati carrying some vegetables. The driver agreed to take him against payment of some money. He quickly embarked into the truck and somehow managed to squeeze through brushing his body with the labours and wedged a seat. The truck smelt of damp, none the less he was glad that he could get rid of the dreadful Nijaraghuli. On his way he saw squatting people in the open field to relieve themselves emptying their bowels.

The parents had a pleasant surprise to see Anjan coming unexpectedly without any intimation. After initial pleasantries Anjan walked straight into his room, He had no sleep and had to travel in a cramped condition. He was so exhausted that he flang himself into the bed and he fell asleep.

In the evening Anjan described the unpleasant incident to parents about the horrific attack on him at Nijaraghuli. Both the parents were panicked. While father consoled him and cautioned him to be more careful in dealing with the rowdy people. The problem with them was that of their ignorance. Mother came near him gave emotional healing by touching the cuts and bruises in his body. Both the parents looked grave and were convinced that Anjan should not go back to that savaged place. Both advised him to pray the authority for a transfer.

Anjan met the Director of Health service and explained the incident to him and prayed for a transfer. To his utter surprise the director was unmoved and was not in no mood to appreciate the gravity of the situation, So much so he was not even bothered to lend a sympathetic ear. Anjan was not sure whether the person on the other side of the table had paid any attention to his story. He pursed his lips and scratched his nose. The Director cleared his throat and said sternly. 'You should not have left the duty in a huff.' He drifted his face towards the window to avoid looking at Anjan and was fiddling with his pen and said 'In simple term that is called negligence of duty. We cannot concede to such requests of self interest. Once we show some leniency in such matter, we will be opening up a flood gate for such requests. Everybody wants to comeout from remote places in some pretext or other.'

After about a fortnight Anjan received a letter from the directorate asking for an explanation why action should not be taken against him for his negligence of duty. Anjan saw no reason to hope that the authority will sympathize with him and consider his prayer for transfer favourably. He however drafted a reply indicating the detail circumstance under which he had to flee from Nijaraghuli to save his life. He prayed for mercy and requested posting anywhere else. But his prayer failed to satisfy the authority and he was suspended forth with. Anjan was disappointed at the unsympathetic behaviour of the director, who was prejudiced with the concept that nobody wanted to serve in remote and backward areas.

He resigned from the job and joined a newly set up nursing home in the city. The parents were initially upset that Anjan had to leave a government job. But there was a consolation that their son will stay with them. Anjan's parents decided for his marriage. They made some queries and searched for a suitable bride for Anjan. However they felt it prudent to take his opinion because he had some affairs earlier.

Anjan was very happy working in the nursing home. Owing to stiff competition the nursing homes in Guwahati were trying to excel in treatments for various critical ailments. The nurshing home where Anjan was working was doing good business and people were getting better specialized treatments. In that context they required qualified specialists and a simple MBBS degree was considered very low professionally Anjan did not have any opportunity to attain post graduate degree in specialized area of treatment. Obviously therefore he was gradually sidelined from the clinical activities and as a result he developed inferiority complex and he felt dejected.

One day his mother on the breakfast table raised the topic of his marriage. She gave a delightful look at Anjan and asked 'As far as I recollect you had an affair with some one a little junior to you in your college. Where is she now? Are you still in relationship? If so, we like to approach her parents formally.'

Anjan did not respond. Obviously he did not have much to say in response. It was about three years he had no contact with Nandita. The misunderstanding had caused all these period of estrangement between them. But Anjan had not been able to completely erase the memory of the days he spent with Nandita. Everything happened out of blue and unexpectedly. All his efforts and logical arguments proved futile to distract her resolute mind. He still believed that it was her sheer persistence that separated them. She obstinately refused to listen to the future. He thought that discussion on this topic with his mother would not be the sensible thing since there was no gleam of hope. Mother looked sad and walked away.

Though the nursing home had several senior doctors yet the administration of the establishment was with a young family member who had a management diploma from some obsecure institution outside the state. Anjan was appointed as deputy manager (administration) and his duty was to manage the day to day affairs of the hospital. Anjan was in charge of the store of medicines as well as spares and disposables. There was a cunning store keeper serving under him who used to sell medicines from the hospital store to the pharmacies situated near by. On several occasions Anjan detected the anomalies and warned him. Unfortunately the store keeper was a close relative of the owner and was acting as a spy. The management had access to confidential information through him. Anjan used to get very much annoyed with him because of his corrupt practices. Eventually his brut candour made him unpopular among the subordinates. Who hatched up a plan to get rid of Anjan. They conspired against Anjan for severe depletion and anomalies in the hospital drug stock. A complaint had been lodged to the management. The management inquired the charges. Several employees appeared as witnesses and vouched against Anjan. The inquiry committee found him guilty of the charges of corruption and negligence of duties and Anjan got fired from his job. From that moment his fate appeared to be sealed. His career was on a downward trajectory. It was a devastating blow to him.

All his hopes of a bright career became elusive and were doomed like shattering glasses. The future looked bleak to him and his self confidence had been completely wrecked. Anjan lost the strength to live to fight another day. Anjan was an agnostic and believed that he was in control of his own destiny had converted into a staunch believer of fate.

In order to escape from the despair he increasingly took refuse in drinking. There were enough reckless people in the surrounding who were readily available to accompany him in his newly acquired fervour. To find a wise and virtuous man is difficult but there are no dearth of malicious peddlers in the society. Anjan was a moderate drinker in the past but as the situation worsened he started abusing.

In the meantime Anjan arranged to sit in a pharmacy as a consultant. He used to charge nominal fees and could earn some money. Birds of same feather flock together. Something happen to him. One by one his drinking partness flocked his chamber and at one time their numbers surpassed the patient visitors and the income severely depleted.

The parents decided to arrange for marriage of Anjan with an earnest hope that he will be rehabilitated and a normal life would be regained. Love and care of wife might play miracle. Anjan also tacitly agreed as he was fully convinced that Nandita was lost for him forever.

But contrary to all expectations there seemed to be no behavioural change in Anjan after the marriage. There was constant stifle between Anjan and his wife and for which the old parents lost all mental peace and they blamed themselves that they were under a curse. Day by day the situation deteriorated to an unbearable state. They were disgusted to see such awful living condition. Finally the parents decided to abandon Anjan and left Guwahati to spend their remaining life in peace in their ancestral town. They suffered from guilty conscience that they made an ignominious mistake and knowingly devasted life of an innocent girl by executing her marriage with their drunkard son. They took refuse in their original town to do penance for the sin they had committed. They started to attend the village prayer hall regularly to seek forgiveness from the God.

(22)

We make a living by what we get but we make a life by what we give

- *Winton Churchill*

Debabrata after his B. Tech from IIT Mumbai had joined a multinational company and posted in Mumbai. Within three years of service he married a local Marathi girl from a respectable family. That was a very confusing experience for his mother who was horrified in disbelief the moment he received the news first. She had no idea how do those people look like, what are their eating habits and social customs. That was very hard for her to reconcile. Nilima Kakati was harbouring some doubts and was hesitant to accept the stranger with open heart.

'Was there any scope for objection for Nilima? Who was she to accept or object?' Nilima Kakati pondered over and reluctantly agreed. She knew her opinions meant little in those things, then.

Both Debabrata and wife Salinee came to Barsila to take blessings from his Mother. All the initial misconception and ill feeling disappeared from Nilima after physically meeting her daughter in law. She was a very intelligent and well behaved girl. Though there was a knotty problem of language yet Salinee could get along well with her mother in law with reasonable ease. Nilima was impressed by Salnee's respect for our age old culture and tradition. For her of course the last words were 'marriage takes place at heaven and she blessed them.

During the visit Debabrata and Salinee were highly impressed by the progress made by the health centre, set up by Nandita. The centre was picking up promisingly. They heaped lot of praise in admimiration of Nandita. The health care centre was a living example of amazing achievement. Determination and tenacity could ensure success and Nandita had amply demonstrated that.

After a few days Debabrata and his wife returned back to Mumbai to resume their respective duties. Salinee carried with her an exhilarating memory of Barsila, the health care centre and of course of beautiful Assam.

After a couple of months all of a sudden a letter reached Debabrata confirming his selection for the master degree course in Stanford university USA. Debabrata was euphoric at the exciting news. He came to his wife with spring foot to show the letter. Both were extremely jubilant. In the evening they came out to marine drive and decided to dine in a restaurant to celebrate the occasion. Standford University located in California state in USA is one of the top esteemed seat of learnings in the world. It was not easy to secure a seat in that university. He was over excited that the university has a few noble laureates as professors there. Therefore to get a chance to study in such a renowned university was like a dream come true for any person. It was a life crave. That was infact a matter of pride for entire Barsila, he thought. But there was no reason for the people of Barsila to celebrate on the success of Debabrata. By then they left bothering for Debabrata and his success was of little concern for them. Debabrata's feelings therefore did not echoed at Barsila.

Debabrata and his wife started to do various calculation on the expenses like travelling, renting of family accommodation at least a studio apartment near by the university, maintenance and then tuition fees. To manage those expenses at least for initial six months they would need a huge sum because he would neither get any fellowship or stipend during those initial days nor saline would be allowed to work during that period, even she could manage to get one. After a basic calculation, they reached to such a figure that taking all resourses available at their disposal is also not enough to meet the expenses and they were still short of a substantial amount. In a conservative estimate they were certain that they will need another two lakhs of rupees more, to be on the safe side, which was about twenty thousand dollars as per exchange rate prevailed at that time.

Banibrata obviously was highly impressed and happy to know the success of Debabrata. He encouraged him. He reminded and quoted a saying of Confucius, 'It doesn't matter how slowly you go as long as you do not stop'. Yes Debabrata was late, he should have done his master degree immediately after he acquired his graduation. 'Ok better late than never. In life one should have high ambition.' He was happy that Debabrata was never detracted from his goal. He was a tenacious and hard working guy. He was convinced.

Banibrata initially was nervous to learn about the money his brother was asking for. Both of them were working as college lecturer didn't mean they had huge bank balance. Banibrata at best could manage about one lakh rupees even after resorting to borrowings from friends. He advised Debabrata to consult with Nandita and seek her advice. Advice was perhaps not the correct word in that context because Debabrata needed no advice. If anything he required was financial assistance to meet his short fall.

Debabrata initially was hesitating to seek help from his sister. because he was fully aware that profit making was not the purpose of the health care centre. It was running as a charity. What ever money generated or come as donations from the people were spent for welfare of the inmates in the centre. After careful thinking at last he decided to consult with his sister thinking if something could be done from her side. Specially by then she had come across with several businessman and who might help if convincingly approached. Finally he decided to write a letter to his sister.

Dear

Nandita,

I am sorry! I haven't written for a long time. In fact I was waiting for a good news and I thought I will write to you after I receive that. Thus the delay. Any way I have been selected for admission into the master degree course in Stanford University of United States of American. This is one among the top universities in the world. Several noble laureates are working there as faculty members. To get a degree from Stanford is itself a matter of great pride. I was craving and praying for my success and God answered my prayer and my dream has come true.

The university informed me that there will no fellowship or stipend for the first six months. As per my information goes I may be able to earn some money to support my expenses by doing some odd jobs only after that proscribed period. I am planning to take Salinee also with me. We will need a considerable amount to take a studio apartment on rent near the university. In a rough estimate we are short of our requirement by about three lakhs to sustain during the first six months including our air fares. I could manage to gather maximum amount of one lakh rupees. So there is a short fall of more about two lakhs. I am now at a fix, unless I can mobilize this money quickly, I am afraid I may loose the opportunity. Dada has assured me of at least fifty percent of my short fall I sincerely hesitated asking you for money, but I see no other option. My immediate necessity is almost one lakh but any extra would be more than welcome.

If need be some unused land also may perhaps be sold or mortgaged which can be retrieved later. So, please do something expeditiously. I will be completely disappointed if I miss this opportunity for non availability of money.

We are in fine health. Hope your health care centre is running well. Convey my regards to maa. Accept my love and best wishes. With warm regards.

Yours

Sarubapu

Debabrata came out of his flat to post the letter. Suddenly he saw people running in front of him as if there was some sprint competition. It's normal in Mumbai, people have to grapple to keep going. Those who fail to cope up with the race are thrown to the winds. It's a competition of survival of the fittest. Everybody men and women, young and old all are in a feat of scurry. He mingled and followed the herd. It was an endless move like a football game without any goal posts. Simply run for the ball. He was weary but can not efford to stop and relax. In the remotely far horizon he saw people playing with gold moving in luxurious car, drinking best of the scots enjoying balad dancing. He was convinced that people were running to fetch all those glittering materials for worldly comfort. A game of treasure hunt. He felt as if somebody was whispering in his ears 'Love of gold cost the greedy man's life.'

Debabrata sat in a bench at the corner of the post office. He looked perplexed. 'Should he ask for money or should not?' He hung back pondering asking for money hurt his self respect but chance for higher study was also something which could not be missed. He knew Nandita had always treated him with deep affection and he had undoubted trust in her. He knew that she would go to the extend possible to resolve his problem. But she had no savings. She had dedicated herself for the society. What help she could extend?' His thoughts met the dead end.

At last he took the letter, pasted the stamps and dropped it in the letter box. Debabrata returned back with a feeling of guilt, feeling of self reproach. But he had the propensity to believe that there was little option left before him. Whom he would approach if not his closest relations. Asking money from her family at this stage might be termed as contrition because instead of extending some financial help to his mother and sister asking from them was a self defeating act, he presumed. He vowed 'I will return all money once I start earning in dollars! Dollars!'

Nandita got up with the sun. Madhabi health centre campus had a wealth of bird life. The birds chirping in the trees in the warm spring sun shine. People reached the clinic from the early morning and wait for Dr. Nandita. She reached the chamber at about nine in the morning. Patients and advice seekers enter one by one to consult with her.

In between the postman entered 'Baideo, you have a speed post letter in your name.' 'A personal letter!' She had a look of surprise and strangely her mind flew for Anjan. There was no apparent reason for her for thinking about Anjan. Since long back there were no correspondences between them. But Nandita could not forget him completely. She know she shall harbour the tenderness for him throughout her lifes. She never expected that Anjan would ever. She broke his heart when she called off the relations. He would never forgive her for her deceitful act. what she could do? She was inextricably involved in her altruistic ideology. She sincerely wished that 'Anjan must be doing very well in his profession and settled respectfully with his family. She was amused to see how swiftly her cherished thoughts sailed towards Anjan.

She opened the letter carefully. If came from Debabrata and her mind drifted to the reality. She quickly read it. Once more she read that. She rummaged through the contents of the letter to find out something. She was peeping into the words. The letter lacked warmth and feeling. She looked terribly upset and sorrowful. A deep sense of despair overwhelmed her.

Sarubapu was in need of money to chase his ambition further. It was obviously justified for him to ask for financial help. She was pleased to learn that Deba secured a seat to study in Stanford University, U.S.A., a highly acclaimed institution the world. One had to be prodigiously sharp in studies to secure admission there. It was a stupendous achievement and was enthralling success.

Debabrata's stunning achievement rightly should have delighted Nandita. But odious thoughts muddled her mind. On one hand Sarubapu's success had elated her and on the other hand his unfeeling behaviour caused pain in heart. She looked forlorn and stood staring emptily into space. She saw some kites were flying high over the sky looking down for prey.

Nilima Kakati felt extremely happy when those destitute ladies came as inmates in the centre she used to spend her time listening their stories of despair. Since then she almost lost all interest on her children. She adored the company of those old ladies in reversal of her reticent behaviour.

Nandita came out of her chamber to hand over the letter to her mother and awaited for a few minutes to know her reaction. Nilima Kakati's face drained of colours. She handed back the letter to Nandita and said with a dull look. 'Sarubapu has done well. He will shine in life.' She stopped and slowly went out of the house to meet the old lady inmates of the health centres. Nandita was sad to see her mother's withdrawn behaviour. Her heart was frozen and a sob caught in her throat. Nandita followed her and went to back her chamber.

Nandita found the letter written by Sarupapa emotionally hollow. He suggested that in order to meet up his requirement some landed property might be sold or mortgaged which was blatantly an act of crude selfishness. She could not digest the mentality of her self seeking brother.

Nandita gave a thought to write back to Debabrata. She be sought him to come once before his departure to United States. 'Mother is still alive and it essential for him to take blessings from her.' She was afraid that she might be swayed away with emotion and might use some unpleasant words thing which might upset Debabrata. So she dropped the idea of writing a letter and instead she decided to send a telegram asking him to 'Come immediately.'

After a week or so telephone in the office rangup. Nandita picked up as usual. Several phone calls used to come to her since morning. Debabrata's voice shook with emotion 'Baideo I have received your telegram. I am reaching home next Tuesday. That means after another five days.'

'Oh!' Nandita lovingly replied 'Thats very nice. Are you coming alone or with Salinee?'

'No. She has to pack things because we are to leave in next couple of days.' Deba was quick to respond.

'No problem, we will be eagerly waiting for your arrival.'

'Hope you are all well'

The conservation abruptly came to an end.

It was a matter of upheaval task for Nandita to mobilise. The huge sunk of money as indicated by Deba. The question of selling or mortgaging of land was out of question. The health care centre seldom received some donations in the form money. Almost everything was in kind. Whatever small amount of money received as donations from well wishers were utilized for paying the employees of the health centre. Her mother had no savings. Nandita was in constant anxiety for finding a solution to Deba's problem.

Debabrata arrived home after a long gap of more than one year. He was wander struck at the progress of the health centre. He never imagined that such an unassailable feat could be transformed into a reality. He originally believed that the project conceived by Nandita was a small venture. But to his utter surprise the project became convincingly big with permanent structures. The health care centre had extensively flourished in these days. The campus is neatly maintained and beautifully land scapped. Ornamental as well as fruit bearing trees planted few years back grown up and the area looked like hermitage of mythological era. He said to himself 'A river cuts a canyon not because of its power but because of its persistence.'

Debabrata was astonished to see that his sister's personality has gone high impressively. She was putting on traditional assamese attire. She was wearing a dark framed pair of spectacles. All these had added to her saintly personality. Debabrata admired his sister for sticking to her dictum. He believed that it was an incredible success story.

Debabrata came for a short duration of one week. Two day elapsed Nandita did not show any inclination to discuss his problem with him. There was no sign of worries in her face. He thought she might not be in a position to solve his problem or she might not be interested to solve it. The cloud of suspicion was hanging over him, because neither his sister on his mother seemed to bother about his problem seriously. He was exasperated at their apathetic concern. Debabrata slowly was losing hope and deep sense of despair started descending on him.

With the passing of days he became impatient and despaired. He had almost given up hope of any fruitful result and was disgusted that Nandita had not realized the gravity and failed to assess the urgency of the situation.

Night descended quickly and the compound of the Madhabi health centre plunged into the darkness. Debabrata was scheduled to leave next day morning. He was bitterly disappointed and went off to sulk in his room after quickly finishing his dinner. Sleep eluded from him because of his anxiety for the future.

Suddenly Debabrata heard mild sound of knocking on the door. He switched on the light and opened the door. Nandita stepped across the threshold with a mysterious smile on her face. He looked at her with startled eyes.

Debabrata had no inkling of the events which might follow next. Nandita had asked him to come with her to her room. Debabrata was baffled why she had called her. He looked blank and walked behind her. Nandita's room was simple but very tidy. This noom looked like a nest surrounded by a tiny world created by her. She had an enlarged photo of their father hanged on the wall and a metallic idol of lord Krishna in an alter placed in a corner where she always lit a lamp and incense stick in the morning. The room was dimly lit.

Debabrata sat on the chair facing his sister who was sitting on the bed. Nandita led the conversation. 'So you are leaving tomorrow' She gave a faint sad smile. 'I could imagine how heretic it will be for you. Take care of your health.'

Debabrata felt embarrassed under her steady obscured gaze. He picked up a pen from the table and was fiddling the same to hide his disappointment. He was increasingly impatient and did not say anything.

'In this health care centre' She gave a glance towards window 'we do not have anything personal. We charge a bare minimum fee to meet our day today expenses.' She gave a pause.

Debabrata simply responded 'Yes, I know that. You are running as a charity.'

She looked pensive and nodded a little.

He was not sure what was there in her mind.

'I fully appreciate your financial problem.' Again after a little pause she said 'I would have been blissfully happy to arrange the required money. But I am afraid how could I do that. You must be very much disappointed.'

Debabrata looked depressed. The words sent him into the nadir of despair. He believed that his expectation hit the end.

'True' She said looking gently to him 'At the same time I must admit and admire your height of success. Opportunities do not come very often. It will be foolish to allow such opportunity to slip out of your hand.'

Debabrata failed to speculate what his sister was driving through. Her expression made him feel obscurely worried. Nandita turned a little and got up from the bed. Debabrata was looking pale and drawn. Nandita took the tangled bunch of key and reached to her wardrobe and turned the key to open the lock. She raked through her clothes and started delving for something. After a little while she came back with a small bag. She did not open it. She sat before him in calm and composed manner.

'I could save a little bit of money during my college days out of my scholarship, savings left over in the post office, which includes money given by dada and mama. I also sold the ornaments preserved by my mother for my marriage. I kept all such savings in this small bag.' She buried her feelings and paused 'If money is not utilized in such occasion what is the value of money'.

She stood in front of Debabrata and she handed over the small bag to him. She smiled faintly and shed tears of happiness. As Debabrata stretched his hand and hold the bag. He was dumb founded.

Tears welled up in his eyes and he desperately faught back his tears. Both of them walked slowly out of her room. The moon peeped out from behind the cloud. Nandita gazed to the sky beyond the moon and smiled wanly. 'I am feeling gratified that small treasure possessed by me as my personal saving is utilized for such a noble cause. I am pleased. The word "My" is vanished for ever from this moment from this compound in the witness of the moon in the sky on this peaceful night.' She gave him a warm glowing smile.

Debabrata struggled to articulate his gratefulness. He gazed at Nandita astoundingly. Her smile illuminated her entire being. Debabrata felt greatly indebted and admired the stupendous generosity of Nandita. At that movement words were redundant. Silence is golden.

(23)

Immortality is to live your life, doing good things and leaving your mark behind

- Shrimanta Sankardev

A storm broke in the late night followed by heavy down pour which lashed the compound of the health care centre. The rain was pouring down in torrents and at times violent. The trees inside Madhabi Swastha Sewa Kendra were violently swaying in the tremendous gast of wind snapped off branches of tree. The storm nearly tore the roof of the house. The brunches of the royal Poinciana tree adjacent to the boundary were fiercey shaking. The storm showed no sign of respite of ceaseless rain. A twigs severed from a tree and the courtyard of the centre was strewn with leaves and twigs. After the down broke the rain ceased and glimmer of sunlight refracted into a faint rainbow in the western horizon.

Nandita comes out and gives a round in the compound. Leaves and tiny branches of trees are scattered all over the front lawn. Lot of birds were nesting in the trees around the health centre. In the fury of the storm a few nests dropped on the courtyard with eggs thrown in the wet lawn. She becomes mournful. She sympathises the pairs of birds who built it with great hope has been razed to the ground. All hopes for raising the chicks have been lost. She catches the sight of one of the birds sitting on a branch looking to the nest despairingly. The songs of the baby birds calling their parents will not be heard any more in the trees. Nandita's mind is completely embroiled by the plight of the birds. She looked pensive and thoughtful.

A bright rainbow has appeared on the west horizon. She has been captivated and has been gazing the stunning beauty of the rainbow. Nandita has thought that there will be no visitors today because the heavy downpour must have wrecked haveoc in Barsila. She is going through a catalogue of some equipments relaxing in her chamber.

The helpers of the centre have come with spades and brooms to remove the debries and to sweep the courtyard. Though cleaned yet the compound is wet and misty.

In the early dawn Anjan boarded into a bus to go to Barsila. Immediately after getting down from the bus he makes a glance to the shops around. He proceeds to a pan shop and enquires if anybody knows the location of Dr. Nandita's Chamber. The bus conductor over hears him and comes running near him. 'Alas! You wanted to go to Baideo's place. You should have told me earlier. It's about a kilometre in the opposite direction. I could have stopped near the centre and drop you right in front of her place.'

In the meantime a few young men who flapping their ears over hear the enquiry of peculiar stranger. One of them cames near Anjan and looks at him. He noticed that the quest looks frail and clumsy. He may be terribly sick and he volunteered to take Anjan on his bicycle.

'No No not required' Anjan has gesticulated by hand refusing the offer, 'you might have some other engagements. Don't worry, I will walk.'

'Don't hesitate, It's quite a distance.' He requested him to sit on his bicycle 'You are coming to our Dr. Baideo's place. She has instructed us to help the sick and infirm persons in bringing to her place. Please come and sit here. He tapped the carrier of the bicycle.

Anjan is amused at the popularity of Nandita. He has thought that she might have done a good practice and earned a lot.

The plaque "Madhabi Swastha Kendra" at the gate of the compound has bemused Anjan and taken aback. The young boy while dropping him pointed to her chamber 'Please go this way. That is

Baideo's office room. In the second half she is available in the office room.'

Anjan has thanked him and staggered inside the premise following the directions given by the boy. He walked through the brick laid approach path both sides were almost covered with equally spaced Devdaru trees. He stood for a couple of minutes on the varandah in front of the door. The Sun is creeping to the western horizon through the patches of cloud. Warm humid air is blowing mildly. Anjan takes a step towards the door. White screen is swaying in the air blown by the ceiling fan. He gathers courage to knock the door.

'Please come in' is the gracious answer from inside.'

Anjan walks slowly into the chamber. Nandita is staggered and her and heart gives her a lurch when she has seen him. Though astounded yet she tries her utmost to remain calm and composed. Anjan has gazed at her with startled eyes and he is completely bewitched by her saintly look. Anjan is worn out and is stooping in font of her. She feels that something must be terribly wrong and she is sad for what Anjan might have endured.

There has been little resemblance with the handsome and promising young Doctor Anjan Saikia with the tired and weary person standing in her front. His appearance is beyond comprehension. Dark shrunken eyes glittered out from a mass of wrinkled frame. His face was almost covered with unkept beard, untidy hair. Nandita recollected how fastidious Anjan was about his dresses and look. Today he has worn a shabby old Jeans and an uncreased T-shirt. Anjan was a shrunken image of his former self.

Nandita standsup from her seat and comes near Anjan. 'What's upto?' Are you ok?' Nandita caresses his hand helped him to sit and asks 'Your health seams to be badly deteriorated. Are you sick?

What's all about, Please feel free to tell me in details what happened to you?'

Anjan is filled with remorse, words failed him. Nandita again has asked. 'Where from have you come?' In the mean time Nandita has asked one girl attendant to bring a glass of water. 'Do not take any tension, the water here is filtered and clean'. Anjan has a quick swill of water and thumps the glass on the table.

'You appear to be utterly exhausted. Don't worry you will be able to take a good rest here.' Nandita is observing his withdrawn behaviour and she put a consoling hand on his shoulder.

Anjan's eyes are on the verge of tears. The sun beam enters though the gap of window screen falls on his nose. He pauses for a breathe. 'Mine is a shattered story, please tell me about your venture'.

Nandita has replied. 'There will be enough time for all these. You will see by yourself. I am craving to know about you, your job your family etc.'

Anjan has sighed deeply and has tried not to let his mind wonder due to his severe frustration. He gives a weak smile and said 'Presently I am like a way farer. I am estranged from the family. You can say abandoned. I As such I have no permanent address.

Nandita puts her hand on his mouth. 'No. Don't be so much down casted.'

Anjan does not remove the hand and enjoyed the sweet smell. He speaks through her fingers 'A fish out of water, no strength to go back to water and swim. All finished. I have given up struggle in despair.'

Nandita has helped him to stand up and helps him to walk upto one of the rooms of her house and requests him to freshen up. She goes out to instruct someone to bring some tea and snacks for Anjan.

He holds the cup of tea and he has shaken his head tiredly 'I was unsuccessful all through. But when I look back I realize that all those terrible things happened to me were not exclusively due to my fault. The ominous fate always betrayed me.' It had it's dangling swords overhead always pointed at me'. He exhaled a deep breathe and said 'My parents, my wife everybody left me due to my unsavoury behaviour. Actually whole of the past episode had been a cruel deception and its not worth describing. You can blame me as a chronic defeatist. The unending failures in my life made me believe in fate and destiny I cursed my bad luck.' Nandita quickly responds. But the truth is that none can destroy iron but its own rust. Like wise no one can destroy a person but his own mindset. She looked as if she might burst into tears any moments.

After a pause Anjan again says 'You knew that I joined as medical and health officer at Nijaraghuli a primary health centre which was running without adequate staff and medicine. I spend two years there. For no fault of mike I was attacked cruelly by group of local people charging me of wrong treatment of a boy who died there. Finally I had to flee from Nijaraghuli. I prayed for a transfer to my Director, but I was out of sympathy and I was suspended. Finally I had to resign from my job.' He couldn't help quaver in his voice. 'Then I joined a local nursing home. Things were moving alright but there also I was targeted by a group of unscrupulous gang of swindlers who hatched a conspiracy against me and finally they were successful in throwing me out from the job.' He has wiped his eyes 'Parents selected girl and I tied the knot with her. But due to my un tolerable incivility mostly under the influence of liquour the innocent girl's endurance crossed the tolerance limit and she left me deserted. My offensive behaviour has brought disgrace to my family. All my dreams gradually eluded from me leaving me utterly frustrated.'

Nandita's heart melted with sympathy to him. It's really a very depressing story. God seemed to be very harsh on him.

Nandita noticed his bitterness. She had never seen a pinch of it in him before. He looked blank, nods his head weekly and again says, 'I did not relish drinking. To hide myself from my failures I took refuse in the drinking and in the process I turned to be a drunkard.' He looks down and said in faltering voice 'My father lost all sympathy to his condemned son. And he abandoned me forever and refused to meet me. The cherished home dreamt by my parents was absolutely devastated.' He has castigated himself for being so stupid.

After a brief pause Anjan continues again 'One day I came to know that my mother left this world' Anjan heaved out a sigh. 'Though she was not by my side yet I always believed that she was the only one who forgave all my appalling conducts and liked to stand behind me. Her memory brings a tear in his eyes. 'I had a feeling of guilt that I had badly disappointed them and made them suffer.' I blamed myself at the thought of all the troubles I had caused to them.'

Nandita has deeply empathized with the unfortunate plight of his life. She has never imagined that destiny could be so cruel to somebody in such a merciless way. Ill fate and bad luck continued to hit this cursed man. Every time he began new move he was impeded by misfortune.

Anjan is happy that after a long period he found some one to speak out his pathetic past to whom he liked the most. With a slight sad smile on his face he again says 'Life is very complex. It is wise not to search its answer, because life changes the question before the answer is found.'

Nandita is visibly upset and her eyes are moisted.

'Anjan' she touches him lightly on the arms. 'I believe you are too tired. Yet you give a glance to my venture.'

She takes him to show the equipments, the laboratory the in door room and the old age centre. Anjan walks with her. He seemed to be amazingly impressed. Nandita takes him to her study. 'This is my study, you can use it as your room. You feel free to ask for anything. There are some books you may relax reading them if you like or you can sleep as well. I will come after late evening. You can stay here as long as you want and visit our centre. You will be able to mitigate your horrific trauma by sharing the sufferings of people who have more dreadful stories to tell. Recall what Napoleon said 'Victory is not always winning battles but rising every time you fall.'

He says nodding his head 'The tragedy of life is in what dies, inside a man while he lives.'

Nandita again is staring glumly into the space through the window 'You meet the patients and interact with them to realize how painful, how terrifying situations they are struggling with. Try to recover your trust. Don't let the sadness and fear of your past to ruin your future happiness. Now try to get some rest.' We will have enough time to talk afterwards.

Anjan does not respond. He shakes his head tiredly. Nandita has left closing the door mildly behind. 'I will join you for dinner. Till then relax.' They exchange relieved glances. Sun is slow descending lower in the sky.

Her love for Anjan has not completely wiped out from her mind. In some remote cranny inside her heart it is still alive and is silently breathing. An intimate relations, physical relation, almost a relation of marriage can't be just forgotten at whims even if they were living far apart for years. She infact had given her heart to Anjan. She was always concerned for him sincerely and wished him to be successful and happy. She comes to her mother to vent out her shocking experience regarding Anjan. She sits near her to describes the incidents 'Ma! Do you remember Anjan?' She looks her mother curiously 'Once I had an affairs with him.'

'Yes' Nilima Kakati nods her head indifferently. 'What happen to him? is he Ok?'

'He has come to meet me here all of a sudden'. Nandita gives a sad sign. He has a long story of horrible misery and he is absolutely devastated and broken down. There is no trace of his glamorous look of past. He could not stick to any job. He became unsuccessful in every effort. He is terribly in traumatic state of mind.' After a little pause she again says 'I will introduce him to you at the time of dinner. Presently I have asked him to take rest for few hours.' I have an inkling in my mind that his life may take a turn if he joins our health care centre.'

Nilima was listening her heedlessly. She is devoid of emotional and feelings. Nandita's mind is still shrouded with sadness. The sun has set and the light has almost gone. Nandita gave a round in her centre and meets the inmates and talks to them in encouraging warmness. All inmates usually eagerly waits for the end of the day when Nandita comes and meets each one of them and enquires their well being and individual comfort. After a few hours the night falls and darkness engulfs the campus. She comes back to her room and await till the time of dinner.

At the dinner time Nandita slowly walks towards the room where Anjan is sleeping. She has reached his room and has knocked the door. The door was not locked from inside and flings open in a little push. She inside and switch on the light. She found nobody there in the room. She suddenly let out a screech in fright 'Anjan! Anjan!' her voice has resonated in the compound. Her voice breaks silence of the compound like sound of shattering glass and the sound jolted the in-mates awake. They have raised to their feet in alarm on hearing the screaming of Nandita. This is an un prescedented happening in the centre. No body ever had such experience. She has rushed to the gate and has shouted loudly' Anjan where have you gone? Please come back.' Nandita feels rumbles beneath her feet.

A few workers come running for her help. She has not bothered about their presence. Nandita stood near the gate and started sobbing. She hastily returns back to the room and is shaking in fear. His ruck-sack is also not there. She shakes her head in disbelieve. Suddenly her eyes meet some paper lying on the table. She runs to grab it. Her heart has started pounding. She flings herself in the chair. She has struggled to regain her composure and has started reading letter with trembled hand.

Dear Nandita,

At the outset my heartiest congratulations on your wonderful success. Words fail me to praise your glorious achievement. I envy your enthusiasm and ardent devotion to your ideology. I started with a wrong concept that success in life is to acquire all material comfort and thought of earning happiness by moncy and power. Ultimately I miserably failed in achieving anything. When I look down memory lake I find myself sploshing in dark pool of misery.

I had strong believe that money is the single most important requirement for happiness. But today I am convinced what Chanuer said 'Money is the root of all evil – always was and always will be.' I am devasted beyond recovery with myraid problems of life.

I was stuck on my journey ahead and was defeated for my inapt handling of situations. After meeting you today I have come to senses, I realize my foolishness. I thought that life is not merely earning from dawn to dusk like the animals. I was blindly under such a misconception and any finally I lost my way. You rightly warned me that we can not be truely happy with selfishness.

Today I have learnt that real happiness and contentment rest in doing for others. Success is when we can bring smile to others. 'There is only one happiness in life to love and be loved,' some great man said that. Lord Budha said 'Thousands of candles can be lighted from a single candle. Happiness never decreases by being shared.'

I am overwhelmed to visit your 'Madhabi Health Care Centre'. May be you had faced many challanges in your journey but you could withstand those with strong resolution and conviction 'All our dreams come true, if we have the courage to peruse them.' I must admit that generosity and selfless service are the best path of happiness.

I was sure that precious memories of our relations did not completely wiped out from our hearts, because till today I am possessing the same intact. All my learnings, my achievements have been eroded and today nothing worthy has been left with me. I became a burden on this world which is a place of hope for many. I have no hope to be happy any more. I have fled two times, first one was for life and the second one is from life.

Time has come to leave now. I have nothing to give you at this hour of farewell except my sincere prayer to God for all his grace to you. Stay always happy and have a long healthy life. May God bless you to be an epitome of selfless service and be an example to many behind us.

I could not gather enough courage to personally meet you to say good bye.

May God be with you.

Bye.

Anjan

A great sense of utter desolation seized Nandita at once. All of a sudden the world seems to have become blank. A sharp fear has descended in her mind. In a moment she burst into tears and started sobbing her heart out. Her mother has rushed in and touched her head. She moved her hand slowly over Nandita's head. Nandita falls right into her mother's arm and goes over sobbing hysterically like an inconsolable baby. Mother has felt her quivering beneath her arms.

Nandita has come out of the room. She has intensely gazed to the sky. The stars twinkling in the sky far away.

She is trying to control the trembling of her legs. She has spotted the bright star and weakly waves her hand and mumbled 'Good bye.'

The only treasure she kept delicately close to her heart has also flown away from her. Tears on her eyes have glinted in the moonlight.